I Want a Coach

With my best
wishes !

Kathleen Bomar

I Want a Coach

Why Coaching is Critical

in the Modern World

MARLEEN BOEN

LEEN LAMBRECHTS

GEORGES ANTHOON

Publisher's Note
This title is also available in Dutch (*Ik wil een coach*, 2012) and French (*Moi aussi, je veux un coach*, 2013).

Authors' Note
Throughout the book, we have tried to take both genders into account with regard to the personal and possessive pronouns. However, where this impeded the flow of the text, we have simply used "he/his".

D/2013/45/325 – ISBN 978 94 014 1109 7 – NUR 808

Cover layout: Peer De Maeyer
Interior layout: Wendy De Haes

Uitgeverij LannooCampus
Erasme Ruelensvest 179 bus 101
3001 Leuven
Belgium
www.lannoocampus.be

INHOUD

INTRODUCTION

What is our image of coaching these days? What are our perceptions and misperceptions?

Professional coaching is not what we frequently see on TV, where people are often shamed into admitting that they are spending too much money or that they are useless in the kitchen. Famous chefs, sports coaches often present a glamorous but sensationalist picture of what it means to coach or be coached—and this has nothing to do with coaching in companies these days.

This is a far cry from the realities of business coaching. The clichés taint our perception and make us too embarrassed to ask for an executive coach. If we don't know what coaching is and the impact it can have on our performance, it will always be difficult to ask for a coach.

What do we, as managers, team leaders or executives, expect of a coach? How do we perceive the benefits of coaching? Often we don't have a clear picture of the coaching profession and hesitate to use coaches to our benefit as both individuals and as a company.

A coach can play an important role in managing the often peculiar relationships between individuals and their companies. Unfortunately, there are many misunderstandings about the importance of coaching in this area.

By providing a definition of coaching we hope to show the way and present a more accurate image of the profession of executive coaching today.

What is the difference between companies today and those of 15 years ago? Is coaching used simply to develop our competencies or does it go further? And if so, how much further? Is coaching just for "fuzzy" managers or is it a real business tool that enables companies to implement sustainable and authentic work processes? Are there any real benefits to being coached? Is it a waste of time? Will I lose face if I hire a coach? What exactly is coaching? Can I openly admit to having a coach? How can it be considered an honour to have a coach? Is coaching an essential investment in the leadership of today?

This book provides inspiration and answers to all of the above questions. Our goal is to dispel the myths around professional coaching and illustrate that it is not so mysterious after all.

CARINE VAEREMANS
– MARKETING DIRECTOR FRIESLANDCAMPINA BELGIE

In today's age, where one (r)evolution chases the other, it is easy to feel disconnected, out of control and as if you have lost your bearings.

Those who would like to take charge of their lives again and determine their own destiny can discover the benefits of coaching in this book. Marleen Boen and Leen Lambrechts cut through all prejudices related to coaching, providing an easily recognizable and no-nonsense outline of the potential that coaching offers for lifelong development both as human beings and as managers. The authors show how coaching can be a tool for continuous and authentic growth … A coach's powerful questions provide an open invitation for personal reflection, growing awareness, trust, inspiration and renewal.

Opting for coaching means choosing quality of life (and work) and expanding your horizons. You are choosing to become the master of your life. You are choosing to follow a compass that aligns with your life's mission.

Coaching leads to better results and to more personal satisfaction.

FREDDY KERCKHOFS
– SALES MANAGER STIHL BENELUX

The quality standards for our appliances are higher than ever, especially as Chinese-made products flood the markets. Yet it is becoming increasingly difficult to find personnel with good technical and commercial skills. The core issues for our sales teams are opening up new perspectives and finding creative ways of looking at our clients.

Letting your own potential emerge, rather than keeping it bottled up, and asking questions that take you out of your comfort zone are key ways to achieve this goal. *Am I prepared to explore the unknown and to take risks with my management style? Am I working on developing my helicopter view and on getting rid of my limiting beliefs? Who is helping me in this process and who makes the necessary adjustments? I often do this without any help or support from anyone.*

It is important to know which management style is needed for each generation to be properly supported. *Am I fit enough to meet that challenge? Can I provide the necessary support and guidance?*

From the very first chapter of this book, Marleen Boen and Leen Lambrechts demonstrate that a coach can add tremendous value, and boost self-confidence, without inducing fear.

Consciously making decisions that satisfy all stakeholders while garnering their support and accepting management's freedom to make decisions is no small endeavour.

Being successful is hard work. I am 51 years old and I believe that I often remain on autopilot without venturing off the well-travelled path, but after reading *I want a Coach* I am ready to look for a real coach who reflects my thoughts and actions. I do not want to merely seek advice and approval.

HANS VAN DER PERRE
– GENERAL MANAGER ATLANTIC BELGIUM

14

The heating and cooling business is going through massive changes. Clean energy solutions demand new competencies of our employees, such as mastering new technologies, as well as discovering and exploring new client markets. We also need to venture off the beaten track and to think beyond common solutions on how our products can be used. Managers in such a demanding field are more grateful to gain clarity. Human capital is more precious and scarcer than ever. It costs a fortune to bring people up to the required skill levels, and without proper attention and motivation we run the risk that our competitors will reap the fruits of our efforts. Looking at the different generations that are sharing the work floor has made me think increasingly about the complexity of this issue. I am ready to take this into account.

Every manager in this company is under tremendous performance pressure, which, in addition, varies with the seasons. Managers in such a work environment are particularly grateful to be granted time to talk to an external coach who listens and encourages them to examine their realities and allows them to be entirely themselves. A coaching programme gives you the chance to rejuvenate your mental energies by looking at your daily concerns through a different lens. Such moments help you to reflect anew on possibilities and opportunities and set a new system in motion. Having the opportunity to address concerns around time management, procrastination, stress, delegation, etc., ensures that the challenges don't get out of hand and become insurmountable problems. This gives our managers the space to take definite decisions that you as the general manager can stand behind.

We can't change the realities of the day, but we can change the way we deal with it and each other.

You will experience the power of questioning first-hand, and you will learn to use and master this skill yourself. This book takes a close look at every type of resistance to being coached, and in doing so helps you better understand the possible benefits of coaching.

Coaching feels good and adds to your quality of life *and* your professional credibility.

MIEKE JACOBS
– EUROPEAN PROGRAMME MANAGER DUPONT PRODUCTION SYSTEM (DPS)

It is the last day of an unforgettable programme about centred leadership in the US and the coach concludes with the words: "With awareness comes the enormous power of choice." Awareness of who you are, of your natural drives, your values and beliefs, the filters you subconsciously use to look at the world, etc., give you the chance to choose how you want to react, how you want to evolve, how you want to grow.

I have been looking for new insights and personal development for as long as I can remember. I viewed it from a purely theoretical perspective, like a life guard who gives instructions from the sidelines, but never puts a toe into the water. It was not until about eight years ago, when I was an executive, that I had the feeling of being stuck in my own fears with a tendency to control everything. As a result, I had reached an undesirable level of stress. Finally I took the step of hiring a coach, what a smart decision! After one conversation we had a whole range of my limiting beliefs on the table. Changing my old beliefs into more empowering ones released untold energy, energy that I could use to take the next step in my personal and professional growth. What this book has made me understand is that growth is a never-ending journey.

May I challenge you to regularly ask yourself the questions in chapter 3? May I ask you to look into the mirror or into the eyes of a coach (often the same effect) and reveal your vulnerabilities?

Effective and authentic people and organisations are change leaders. But engaging in effective and authentic relationships, I believe, begins by creating a deep awareness of the self.

JOYCE PAFORT
– CORPORATE HUMAN RESOURCES DIRECTOR RANDSTAD

18

I WANT A COACH

When talking about employee development in companies we often think of all types of training. That can certainly be the answer for specific learning objectives: for acquiring special knowledge, for instance, or for learning new skills. However, the key to a deeper development of an individual lies in a more personalised approach, especially when it comes to functioning in a more complex environment or for people in leadership positions. That's when we talk about *coaching*. You learn to look at your environment and people's behaviour from a different perspective, which leads to greater awareness and the understanding that you have the choice to see and do things in more than just one way.

As an HR manager and coach, I believe that individual coaching can make an important difference for all employees and thus for the entire organisation. This is true in particular for all those who are in the middle of their careers. *Who am I? What am I capable of?* and *What do I want?* seem to be the questions that come up even more frequently at that stage of our lives, and they defy easy answers. Randstad, as an HR service provider, aims also internally for sustainable employability. Lifelong learning is considered the key to a successful career, both within a company and outside of it.

Now that I have completed the certified coaching training, I have come to better understand the power of individual coaching. This book removes all preconceived notions about coaching. It is a must-read for anyone who is searching for a way to gain greater awareness about their work—especially in today's challenging context, in which many companies are looking for their added value and how they can make that difference.

19

SONIA VERMEIRE
– MANAGING DIRECTOR PUBLICARTO

As an advertising agency, we have a challenging role to play in a tremendously altered media landscape that requires a completely different approach. Instead of simply translating the needs of an advertiser into the ideal media mix, we now have to master the art of reacting more creatively to consumer signals and, even, to create consumer needs. Such a mentality switch also requires a different management style.

It is no longer a question of, 'You ask, we deliver.' As an executive you have to ensure that your team remains intellectually challenged.

As I was reading *I Want a Coach* I got the feeling that, as a manager, you do not have to ride this change process alone. A professional coach can serve as a sounding board, without passing judgement.

This book, with its wealth of concrete questions and practical case studies, will inspire you to challenge yourself and to open yourself up for self-reflection.

I am convinced of the value of coaching and am following a coaching programme called 'People Focused Management' to find my own answers and to improve my performance and that of my team.

Els verhoyen
– Senior manager ing belgium

Managing seems simple. Managers communicate the vision of the company and make sure that their teams do their jobs in accordance with that vision.

However, to get people to 'do what they are supposed to do' is not so easy. Authoritarian leadership is no longer accepted. The times of giving commands, obediently following orders based on a dialogue model of "Why?" "Because I said so" are long gone. Today's leaders have a new task: to inspire. They must convince and rally support for a common vision. They have to ensure that people do their work with enthusiasm.

Coaching has helped me to truly implement this insight in my work.

I used to have the tendency to quickly and efficiently find my own solutions. After all, with all my years of experience I surely knew the answer to each problem that came up, right? Since then I have learned that going into 'asking mode', taking on a calm attitude and truly listening to the opinion of the people around us, especially our employees, not only ensures more buy-in, but also leads to better results.

My coach taught me to listen actively and empathically, to see situations through the eyes of my employees more often. Showing that you can see the world from their vantage point - their concerns and their perspectives—grows the kind of recognition and appreciation necessary for an open and positive work environment. Moreover, employees who you really listen to, can give you an enormous amount of information and insights. This allows you as a manager to adjust expectations and assumptions, and to succeed.

I Want a Coach opens up a whole new world, based on humility and reflection. Quality managers are in fact able to show themselves to be vulnerable. They are critical, primarily towards themselves. A good manager knows to take a step back, to take the necessary distance, even with regard to the realisation of his own dreams, his own successes and failures. He has a good understanding of his own strengths and weaknesses, as well as his fears. This is a great feat, which not everybody is able to accomplish alone. Being accompanied by a coach in this process is therefore crucial.

Coaching is a fantastic gift; an essential tool for self-development and reflection. The acquired skills stay with you and can be used again and again. For that, this book is an outstanding guide.

1

Why is there a need for coaching?

PART 1

WHY IS THERE A NEED FOR COACHING?

Internationalisation, globalisation, computerisation: the competitiveness of companies is suffering constant pressure. In order to survive, companies need to be proactive, make quick decisions and be as agile and flexible as possible. To maintain your position as company leader or manager in this context is not granted. Previously there was only one boss who was always right. Things have changed. The traditional company hierarchy makes way for decentralised matrix structures where leadership is scrutinised, and as a manager you are under constant fire.

In order to function properly in this context, more and more managers consult professional coaches. These coaches act as a sounding board, they offer different perspectives and contribute to making the decision process a pleasure instead of a burden.

Furthermore new company values and trends often give rise to fear and insecurity. Coaching in these circumstances – which are looked at further in this chapter - is often the facilitating factor for both company leaders and employees.

I. MANAGERS IN TODAY'S WORLD

1. FAREWELL TO THE BOSS

The days when 'the boss' was the only smart kid around are over—and the manager who thinks he needs to be able to do it all himself will find his image tarnished. It used to be: The boss knows it all, can do it all and finds solutions for everything; he makes decisions, his word is the law and the rest of the company must follow.

In the days of patriarchal family businesses and tightly run enterprises, this approach often worked well. Leadership was never questioned, certainly not as long as the results were satisfactory. In situations like this, a coach cannot offer much, if any, added value.

However, in today's business environment an authoritarian leadership style will not get you very far. Younger generations no longer buy into it. They have become outspoken, they have studied longer and they are far more independent thinkers. In today's enterprises, we therefore find much more room for other voices to be heard.

The model of the dictatorial patriarch works as long as employees have the sense that their leader takes care of them, that he provides security. The pitfall is that this type of leadership is heavily vested in a particular person. We often see that when the patriarch leaves or is replaced by other managers, the trust of the employees disappears with him—with dire consequences.

Small/medium-sized enterprises and multinationals have changed considerably. Who is in fact at the helm of these organisations? Managers, shareholders, steering committees are often unknown entities to their employees, and yet, they impose one truth and one vision on their workforce. The bad news is: not everyone agrees.

We are moving from a directive style towards a more visionary form of leadership. Managers are expected to support their people while ensuring that employees enjoy their work and remain committed to the company's vision.

Each employee speaks his own language and has his own reality and vision. The executive of today is flexible and able to understand and respect the perceptions and truths of his employees. At the same time, he manages to rally his employees behind a common company vision. In other words, for companies to be successful they need managers who are open to different ideas, managers who, by somehow integrating those ideas into a strong, all-embracing vision, manage to engage their employees, inspire them and motivate them from the core rather than imposing the law from the top down. This is no easy task, especially as the manager has to rely entirely on himself in finding and mapping out the way.

Entrepreneurship and ownership

With the gradual disappearance of authoritarian leadership styles we see a new trend in which employees are increasingly asked to display greater entrepreneurship and ownership within a company. Entrepreneurship stands for *taking initiative and starting new projects*. Giving ownership means asking *employees to handle their projects as if they were working for themselves and to make decisions as if for their own business*—with an eye towards optimising resources and time.

It is all very well for managers to expect entrepreneurship and own-ership. However, are the managers equipped to deal with it? Will they be able to manage this process?

If a company is not ready to embrace these values with enthusiasm, employees may quickly turn their backs on the organisation.

Ilse, office manager, 28

I am launching a new structure, as is expected of me. Management thinks it's a great idea and is fully behind me, but when it comes to the implementation, I am getting resistance from all sides and everyone is suddenly pulling back. Do I really want to go through with these changes? Is it not management that needs to change?

Often companies feel the need for change and attract staff, young professionals who have the proper entrepreneurial and ownership skills to innovate, for this purpose—but the companies themselves can be inept in handling change. Their young and eager talents suffer burn-outs. If the companies they work for are not sufficiently ready to transform, these young employees get quickly disillusioned.

"I am going to hang in here for another couple of years, learn what I can, gain a bit more experience and then I will go into business for myself." Comments like these are heard more and more often. What, then, are we doing as companies? We are losing our precious human resources at an increasingly younger age. First we invest in our people and then we chase them away. It seems that our young talents are not getting the leadership they need.

How are you as a manager going to embrace and promote the initiatives of your employees? And how are you going to guide them without losing their enthusiasm? Your task as a manager is to stimulate good ideas while ensuring that your employees stay on board.

This is where coaching comes in. Using a coaching attitude in dealing with your employees presumes that you honour their values. You guide them by asking questions and not by imposing your truths on them, you remain open to their opinions and give them feedback in a respectful and honest fashion. If you are successful in this approach, your employees will feel appreciated and inspired to take the initiative—and you reduce the risk of losing them. In other words, training managers how to deal with the entrepreneurial spirit of their employees in a coaching manner can only pay off.

There is something else: allowing your employees to launch and implement a marvellous idea takes a great leap of faith. For many managers, to rally behind an employee's initiative simply goes a step too far, and suddenly all kinds of barriers rear their ugly head: fear of losing face, endangering your position, jealousy ... These feelings are only too human, but they stand in the way of the evolution of your company, the growth of your employees and your personal development.

Respect for the truths of your employees

Transforming limiting fears into an empowering and stimulating mindset can be achieved through coaching. The inherent personal and trust-inspiring approach of coaching makes it safe for you to expose your weaknesses and discuss your concerns, both as a person and as a manager. It is the only way to let go of your fears, improve your coaching skills and fulfil your own growth and development goals.

A coach accompanies the manager in the search of his own added value. How can he approach employees to get results? How can he motivate people based on their needs to achieve the desired performance?

Coaching means *broadening perception*. A coach helps executives to look at things through the eyes of their employees and other stakeholders rather than solely through their own lens. With this type of support, teams can work along the same lines, for if you have seven employees you will find seven different ways of looking at the same problem.

As an executive you can no longer expect your employees to accept your thoughts and ideas outright. You need to display a different mindset, one that permits you to ask your employees' opinions and then, of course, to take them seriously. This means you need to take a step back from your own beliefs.

Unlearning that you are the sole keeper of the truth can be a difficult process. A coach is the perfect sounding board in this process and the ideal facilitator when transitioning from traditional management to a new way of leading.

Footprints that speak volumes ...

While doing research for this book, I stumbled upon a cartoon that shows what type of leadership is needed today.
The cartoon perfectly sums up the evolution of leadership through the centuries and shows the way we are heading.
In the image, the animal footprint stands for the 'survival of the fittest', which was useful in the days when pure (animal)

survival was the priority. The footprint of the first human indicates the period when humans began to harness animals and the fruits of nature. The heavy-duty footprint refers to a command-and-control style that reigned during the evolution of the "enterprise" concept. The imprint of the heel of a woman's shoe refers to what recent management literature terms the "emotionally intelligent leader", which women are supposedly more inclined to be. Whether this is true or not, those (men or women) who want to be successful today, to be authentic leaders, must understand that the way to success includes as many EQ as IQ elements.

Georges Anthoon
previously HR Director at AXA, currently executive coach and mentor

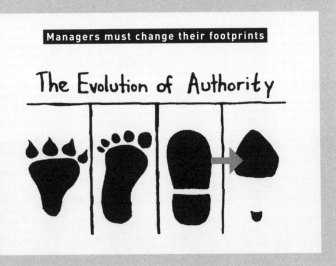

2. KNOWLEDGE AND EXPERTISE ARE NO LONGER ENOUGH

It is not enough to be the smartest kid on the block. In other words, it is no longer sufficient to know our business inside out or to have great expertise in our field. The days of depending on the expert manager are waning since employees today often know more than their executives.

With the internet and social media gradually evolving as a source of primary knowledge, employees are sometimes more up to date on the latest developments than their bosses. Consequently, managers are increasingly valued less for their knowledge and need to become a different kind of leader. This has led to a trend toward more authentic leadership. We are in search of new parameters; i.e. new ways to earn respect. Dealing better with "not knowing" or "not having to know everything" comes up frequently in coaching.

Managers are more often expected to make decisions in areas with which they are not familiar. A CEO who has to make an important IT decision will put his company's fate into the hands of the CIO. Yet, due to rapid developments in the ICT sector, a decision made today could prove costly tomorrow. If, for example, in 2010 you decided to buy a server that was due to come out in March 2011 for your small/medium-sized business, your decision might have turned out to be too costly, complex and obsolete as the far cheaper and more accessible cloud computing had by that time eclipsed old technology and made owning your own server redundant.

Top managers must therefore be able to make decisions based on the insights of experts. But those insights also need to be linked to the real needs of the company and its core business. A visionary manager needs clarity of thinking and the ability to see the big picture. Merely *knowing your business* is no longer enough to be a leader. Even small/medium-sized businesses are facing this reality.

Life has become more complex than ever. Today it is no longer possible to check up on all the facts yourself, you will want to trust your employees and dare to make decisions without having all the details.

3. HELICOPTER VIEW

As we can see from the above, today's manager needs a helicopter view. As a visionary manager you are successful if you have the ability to keep an eye on the big picture and not get lost in all the nitty-gritty details of your business. This requires keen observation of yourself, of your market and of your employees.

In addition to being a good observer, managers need to be creative in conveying their findings with enthusiasm. Managers are expected to have the ability to express their conclusions in an inspiring and personal fashion to ensure that everyone feels involved and valued.

Managers who continue to micromanage will drown due to a high workload and will be unable to take inspired decisions. To make decisions that allow a company and its people to grow, you need to be able to stand up for your positions with conviction, while trusting that everyone is doing his job to the best of their ability and that all the necessary details are taken care of.

Trust cannot be learned in a training course. Trust presumes good self-knowledge, knowledge of others and the ability to make sound judgements.

And yet many of us are afraid to work from a place of trust (as opposed to a place of control and distrust). These fears are often based on our experiences because we have all witnessed abuses of trust every now and then. We often use that as an excuse to work from a base of distrust. That is how we become control freaks, forgetting about the countless times when giving trust served us well. But what does being in control bring us? How do you deal with the extra workload if you want to be in charge of everything?

4. HIGH EXPECTATIONS

Employees often have high expectations of their managers. When things don't go well, the manager gets the blame. As a manager you are *it* and you are considered to be a role model. People are harsh with each other, and certainly with their managers. After all, managers earn higher salaries.

And so it can get very lonely at the top. Managers therefore need self-confidence, solid decision-making skills and a healthy dose of self-esteem, none of which can be taken for granted. That is why good advice, a sounding board, a person whom you can trust and with whom you can share your doubts, is priceless.

Lonely at the top

During my time at global investment, retirement and insurance group AXA, I had the opportunity to assess many of the group's CEOs and executive directors across Europe. What struck me was how self-assured, even quite macho behaviour in the beginning of the interview frequently gave way to confessions about their own doubts and fears as the conversation continued. Concerns about their work and their future were key topics: *Where am I going with my career? What plans does the company have for me? What will the economy and my future bring? How much longer will I be able to cope with a job that is focused mainly on numbers and efficiency? Will there ever be an end to the pressure of 'doing more with less'? What do people think of me as a leader? How will I ever achieve greater balance in my life?*

What came up in the discussions was the need for these leaders and managers to discuss their doubts and fears with someone they could trust. They suddenly showed their human side and expressed their desire to voice their doubts, plans, ambitions, fears and problems in an environment in which they could be themselves and did not need to play the hero. Coaching provides for such an environment.

Those who have never had to deal with executives and senior managers might find themselves thinking what wonderful and rich lives (literally and figuratively) these people must have. They do, and they don't. Behind the facade of success, we often find much sadness and insecurity, as well as guilt about all the things they would like to accomplish but haven't, such as paying greater attention to themselves (hobbies, rest and relaxation) or spending more quality time with their partners, children, friends.

As a coach of a number of CEOs and senior managers, I often hear that they feel rather lonely at the top and thus are happy when, every few weeks or so, they have the chance to exchange thoughts with a person they can trust, someone who can help them see things from a different perspective.

They enjoy the fact that they may reflect, together with the coach, on their own thoughts, beliefs and decisions in a completely different way, even discovering their own blind spots. In the beginning, this is a painful exercise, but over time they realize the enormous opportunities their new insights can afford them. Once they have reached that stage, they feel triumphant about their newly chosen personal changes.

J.K. Rowling, the author of the Harry Potter series, once said: "You don't need magic to change your life; all the necessary powers lie within you."

There is hardly a better way to describe the effects of coaching: a coach, armed with an arsenal of open questions and the competencies to reflect your blind spots, helps you discover different aspects of yourself, which in turn helps you to move on successfully.

Georges Anthoon
previously HR Director at AXA, currently executive coach and mentor

The high expectations that we have of ourselves

We want it all, and more, financial security, a flourishing career, an interesting job that affords us enough free time for ourselves, for our families, for our relationships. Moreover, we want the perfect house, the latest car, fantastic holidays, smart kids who are involved in sports and all things cultural. We are overwhelmed by the options life offers these days.

Does the fulfilment of all these desires really make us happy? How can we, among all those options, identify our personal vision of happiness? Do we know what we really want? Or is our sense of happiness drowning in a sea of material comfort?

Liesbeth, 35

I have a five-year-old child. I get up at 3:15 am to get the household in order before going to work. Otherwise, I won't get it all done. A second child is out of the question. We wouldn't manage financially. There will never be enough of anything.

You will come across this sort of account frequently, in both less and more extreme forms. The key here is to be able to make choices without being afraid that *I'll lose too much*. Often, *much* refers to financial or material things. Do you have the courage? Do you dare leave materialism behind as the only form of happiness and look for joy in other places?

Here the need for coaching comes in again; it can help you gain greater awareness of yourself and of your deeper values and true desires. Coaching teaches you to make more conscious decisions, ones that fit you and make you happy. This allows you to search for joy beyond the world of materialism and comfort. You might find a deep sense of happiness, a happiness that truly satisfies your desires.

Coaching leads to a deepening of your sense of self, something that is becoming increasingly important in our lives. Levels of prosperity in the developed world have risen, and more people demand the right to greater prosperity (greater material comfort). But will that make them happier?

More self-awareness is needed, which means being more realistic about our competencies, how we spend our time, our work schedules, etc. When we realise that each of us is in a different place and we do not all have the same opportunities, we can make more conscious choices that suit our needs and make us truly happy.

You learn that it is okay to make use of a coach at work to help you become more true to yourself, at least in the workplace. If becoming true to yourself happens to affect your private life as well, your employer is lucky, because "happy people are productive people".

5. THE SEARCH FOR GREATER FULFILMENT IN LIFE

People want more than just financial reward for their work. Money alone does not satisfy. We all look for fulfilment in life. Until recently, success tended to be measured by one's level of material possessions, the classier car and bigger house were common signifiers of success.

This benchmark still applies today. It seems that one model of perfection, success or happiness rapidly follows on the heels of another. We hardly have time to adjust, to adapt to the new norms, and we often feel lost. For without those parameters, do we know who we are? What gives sense to our existence? What do we work for? A salary rise tends to increase happiness only marginally. Deep inside we feel a call towards something else. But what? What is it that gives us true satisfaction?

As a manager you are often confronted with this question. Do you want to use and develop your talents? Would you like to live according to your intrinsic values, to live at a more profound level? Do you wonder how much meaning your work adds to your life? Are you still sure about where you want to go with your career?

The answers to such fundamental questions are not always obvious and require greater introspection. And the road to real answers is not straight (or straightforward), but a road full of twists and turns, with pitfalls and bumps and the risk that you will run in circles.

Having a trustworthy guide is thus not merely a luxury. A coach accompanies you in self-reflection, guiding you towards a suitable answer to the questions above, adding meaning on a personal and a professional level.

Career counselling and coaching are increasingly common in companies. In their search for greater fulfilment in life, employees want to know how they can develop their careers in a meaningful way. Managers, as well as employees, are opening up to self-reflection and want to be coached in introspection. Self-reflection is an inextricable part of our evolution today. There is no way around it.

II. CHANGED EXPECTATIONS

The previous section described the various aspects of today's business environment that present managers and executives with new and more complex challenges and expectations. These new patterns are, of course, closely linked to societal trends. We shall examine a few of these trends and explore what role coaching can play in each of these scenarios.

1. WOMEN ARE BECOMING MORE SUCCESSFUL

Although the glass ceiling remains, women are increasingly making their way to the top echelons of corporations, a trend that seems to have gathered momentum in recent years. While we can only celebrate such an evolution, the road to success is, even in these emancipated times, still very demanding for many women.

Women can find it difficult to assert their presence in management teams and on executive boards, where men usually represent an overwhelming majority. Many men still have a hard time accepting a woman as an executive.

Coaching can be useful in removing prejudices that both men and women may have about each other. It can also teach them how to adopt a coaching mindset when dealing with one another. The business can thus develop a more open vision with regard to career chances for female and male professionals and gender equality. Creating a climate that promotes a healthy curiosity about the different angles and perceptions among the genders also creates a win-win situation for the company. The first questions would be: "What can we learn from each other?" "How can we contribute, regardless of our gender?" The outcome is always enriching.

2. FROM TIME AND STRESS MANAGEMENT TOWARDS TIME PERCEPTION

Time management as such is obsolete. The issue today is how we can best use the amount of time available to us. How conscious are we about the use of our time? How strictly do you separate work time from private time? Do you use your private time to do work and vice versa? (For example, should reading work-related emails in the evening be considered work?) The blurred lines between work and private time often cause us a lot of stress. What are we to do?

To begin with, we need to dismiss the notion that stress is bad. There will always be stress. The question is rather: how do we deal with stress? The first lesson is to learn how to look at your situation calmly. It is a matter of us making a conscious decision to remain serene among the complexity, both on a personal and professional level, and both as an individual and as a society. To reflect on your use of time it is necessary to slow down. This is the only way to get to the bottom of the deeper thoughts and feelings that motivate you.

3. RAPIDLY CHANGING TIMES

Change is happening more and more quickly. Reorganisation, fusions and mergers are increasingly a part of daily business. You are working in company X and before you know your way around, you are suddenly part of company Y—with all that implies: new bosses, new rules and new colleagues ... With each change you need to adapt and go with the flow. Of course, things will improve—at least, that's the promise. But does it really feel that way? Will things really improve?

Whatever the case, when two corporate cultures come together it is always difficult to find common ground. Training and coaching are indispensable here. The first candidates for coaching are the managers themselves, they need to be role models.

It may not be easy as a manager to admit that you too are grappling with the new situation and that your adaptability seems to be challenged at times. How prepared are you really to do what is necessary to achieve results while also making people happy?

An external coach plays an important role when it comes to acclimatising managers and employees to a new culture. As a manager you often don't have the luxury of time. In addition, chances are that the impartial perspective of an external person will be more readily accepted than that of someone within the company who might be seen as having his own agenda.

An external coach encourages people to examine *themselves* instead of analysing the culture or the organisation. He inspires them to map out their own paths of development, giving meaning to the new culture. He points out the blind spots of employees in a non-judgemental manner which is of immense value for those who want to weather the storm all the changes bring about. Securing a tangible amount of self-knowledge and awareness of one's abilities and limitations is therefore not an extravagance.

If you are not prepared to develop greater self-awareness you will have regrets in a few years' time. Even if you are competent, you will not have the skills to react to change and successfully adapt. Sooner or later, you will find yourself at a dead end.

Quite often we are in a state of slumber. We work hard and are always busy; we live on autopilot. Our routines keep us going, and this can be a good thing, but they also diminish our level of alertness, flexibility and our awareness.

A perfect example is how we react when we are unexpectedly fired. People cannot understand how they can be cast aside, just like that. It is a bitter pill to swallow. For some, such an event turns into a real trauma, making it difficult for them to continue with or regain their professional careers.

People with greater self-awareness are better equipped to pick up changes in their surroundings. They are more receptive to signals from their environment and more likely to see the writing on the wall. Of course, it is never easy to lose one's job, but those who have operated from a higher level of awareness can survive and give these events their proper place. This allows them to move on.

The responsibility of expanding your awareness is all yours. You have to be prepared to roll up your sleeves and get to work. Coaching, however, is an instrument that guides you. A coach will use questions and confrontation techniques to help you on your path to gaining greater awareness and learn how to turn a situation to your advantage instead of getting stuck in resistance. This is how coaching helps build self-confidence.

Just do it

Michelangelo once said: "Every one of us has a masterpiece inside, and it is up to us to discover it."
The higher up on the company ladder you are, and the more decisions you are making there, the more important it becomes to talk about your potential. However, it is not easy to keep growing, both as a person and as a professional. It is precisely in moments of crisis that external help can work wonders and help you come back to yourself. These moments represent exceptional opportunities for personal growth and/or improvement of the present.

However, for sustainable change, insights must be followed up by actions. Once we know what we want, what we need to develop and in which direction we should march, we need to "just do it". This is, of course, the well-known slogan of sporting goods company Nike. A pair of new sports shoes or a flashy outfit does not turn us into super athletes. You have to do the work. Ambition and drive help you at the start of your journey, but after a while you run the risk of losing momentum. This is when external help from friends or from the local fitness coach can do wonders, by motivating you and by reflecting your lapses back at you.

An executive coach plays a similar role. Many coachees begin their chosen professional and/or private journey with enormous enthusiasm and good intentions, only to fall back into old habits and ways of thinking ... A short visit from their coach can help to put them back on track ...

4. KNOWLEDGE IS NOT THE ONLY ROAD TO CERTAINTY

Our theoretical and mental models are becoming out of harmony. We rearrange models to better understand reality and to be reassured, only to realize that there are numerous other ways of looking at our realities.

Past 'certainties' are crumbling, while traditional science is being questioned. Look at the results of the field of quantum physics! According to some conclusions, the observer of a study influences its outcome merely by watching the experiment—what Schwartz[1] calls the 'Zeno effect'.

'Knowing' is no longer a foothold. Of course, this is not the first time science has been questioned. Every 40 years or so, new books come out that challenge science as we know it. In the past, aspects such as emotions, intuition and the subconscious were often dismissed because they were difficult to interpret scientifically. Today we are slowly beginning to understand that we need to consider these elements in our analyses of human beings, society and business. And coaching does.

5. AN INCREASE IN PSYCHOSOCIAL DISORDERS

Rapid change can lead to much stress and frustration, and the final step to full burn-out is often small. Psychological illnesses are the fastest growing disorders in our society. This is to a large extent due to how we deal with 'threats'. Are we sufficiently equipped for the 'dangers' in our society? Do we have enough resilience to withstand setbacks? A sudden dismissal, a colleague's emotional outburst, a promotion that slipped through our fingers, an impending divorce, children with learning challenges ... we are ill-prepared for such events. We either flee or freeze. If we don't manage to shake off the paralysis we create traumas which block our ability to (re)act. We are unable to demonstrate the required flexibility to cope with the new situation. We remain stuck in our old patterns. We block ourselves.

Coaching can help break through these old patterns and help us look at the situation with different eyes. New or different options unfold, and we can choose how to react. Even if we do hold on to our old thought patterns, we are aware that we have made a conscious decision to do so, rather than being dominated by subconscious mechanisms. Our level of awareness determines how well we develop.

If you don't listen properly to your frustrations and don't deal with them on a deeper level, you run the risk of suffering from burn-out, depression or cardiovascular illness. People like to hold on to their own truths— this is the easiest and most comfortable path. However, by doing so we diminish our ability to fight the anguish that so often follows from holding on too long to truths that no longer serve us.

A coach empowers us to take responsibility in our search for a way out of the misery and helps us understand that we can choose how to deal with whatever happens to us.

Executive coach Marie

In my coaching practice I repeatedly encounter managers and CEOs who are stuck in their own truths "about the others". Their complaints about what others mess up, don't understand or fail to do can seem endless. When I point out that their complaints reflect their own unfulfilled needs, they are often surprised. When I hear that they take their frustrations out on their employees, I get worried. With such behaviour you are not a role model for others. Instead you confirm and encourage the idea that it is okay to complain about others and to avoid addressing employees directly.

Of course, managers want the chance to vent their dissatisfaction from time to time, but that shouldn't be done with just anybody. A neutral person needs to be on hand. This is why coaches are indispensable. Your coach listens to your frustrations, mirrors them back and questions them. He invites you to gain new insights, to look at situations differently, and to take appropriate action.

People who are trying to deal with many complexities while at the same time suppressing their frustrations are constantly performing a balancing act. Burn-out is much like a physical cramp, your body can no longer cope with the demands of what your mind wants to achieve.

Coaching helps you to regain your equilibrium by expanding your perceptions and creating a deeper self-awareness. Having a clear understanding of yourself, your choices and their consequences helps heal the paralysis and allows you to function more freely and with greater flexibility.

A study by Jan Ramsoy and Sigrid Sover Kjeldsen reveals that the stress levels of 111 clients who were coached for 10 hours had dropped by up to 18% after a three-month period. Some participants even reported a stress reduction of nearly half (48%) their initial level.

Stress (and of course, burn-out) leads to absenteeism. Supporting employees in dealing with stress therefore lowers levels of absenteeism. Ramsoy maintains that an organisation that manages to reduce the rate of absenteeism in 100 people by 1% will save the annual salary of one FTE.

The graph below shows the percentage of respondents who said that coaching had a positive impact in the areas indicated.

Effects of coaching in connection with stress at work

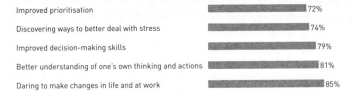

Improved prioritisation — 72%

Discovering ways to better deal with stress — 74%

Improved decision-making skills — 79%

Better understanding of one's own thinking and actions — 81%

Daring to make changes in life and at work — 85%

From Trapeze Artist to Juggler

Suppose you end up in the top echelons of a company only to ask yourself: "What am I doing here, for goodness sake?" This is exactly what happened to Erik Dejonghe, the former CEO of Barco (1982–2001). He decided to step down as CEO because he had twice suffered from burn-out. Today he regularly gives interviews in which he talks openly about his doubts and his struggle at the helm of Barco due to the extreme pressure from shareholders, clients, competition and employees.

Perhaps his most impressive quote is this: "If you work as a trapeze artist in a circus and you are becoming afraid of heights, it's probably time to do something else. You might want to consider becoming a juggler."

Those who have the feeling that they constantly bump up against their limits need to dare take a closer look at reality. External coaches can be of enormous help in this process by removing our blinkers and helping us to discover new goals that are better suited to us.

Today, Dejonghe is an independent education management consultant and an active visiting professor in universities; a different life which fits him like a glove.

6. LONGER WORKING LIVES

A career today ends later than it did for the previous generations. This trend is gaining currency throughout Europe, leading to the following:

> Until recently, early retirement from active professional life used to be the rule; today it is the exception. Today, at 50, you can expect at least another 15 years of working life. Even at this age, you must be in top form on the work floor, welcome change and embrace new technologies.
> For many people, this requires huge effort, and turning to a coach in these late stages of a career can be extremely valuable.

> For the first time ever, we see four different generations on the work floor. Getting them to work together smoothly is no small feat. Statements like, "Today's youth think they know better" or, "The old folks think they can boss us around" are evidence of misunderstandings and distrust. It goes without saying that such attitudes are not exactly conducive to the growth of a business. As long as each generation remains intransigent about their views, there will be little room for development. Coaching helps to break through prejudices and in the process fosters better relations. With coaching, we see that each generation has its own vision, strengths and development issues, and that the different generations can learn much from each other.

III. THE BENEFITS OF COACHING

The aforementioned trends—more women becoming more success-ful; a move from time and stress management towards time percep-tion; continuous and rapid change; a world in which knowledge no longer means certainty; an increase in psychosocial disorders; and a longer working life—are symptoms of a rapidly changing society. They require of us the capacity for greater self-awareness if we want to stay on top of all new developments. This applies even more so to executives because only an executive who has a strong relationship with himself can deliver his message with integrity and conviction.

The question is: which sources can we tap into to discover (or redis-cover) our potential, or purpose? *Introspection* is indispensable but in the process we often bump up against a few self-judgements. As a result, the path to inner peace is often erratic, filled with potholes and sky-high obstacles. It is possible for an executive to embark on this quest alone, but, from experience, the results are usually unsat-isfactory. We often end up doing little more than repeating old habits or techniques for finding ourselves, such as taking a holiday, instead of tapping into new sources of inspiration.

Colleagues may be another resource we can tap into. Executives have a great need for openness among fellow executives, a potential to learn from one another—but that requires honesty. How honest can we be with a colleague or manager? There are other barriers too. Which sides of ourselves would we rather hide? Are we addicted to our own way of doing things? Are we blind to the benefits of seeing other points of view? Can we allow ourselves to be vulnerable?

Coaches are experts in guiding this quest for rediscovery, or renewal. Through powerful questioning and honest confrontations, they invite us to reconnect with our inner power and to strengthen it.

Vulnerability: Obama's leading by example

When you ask managers who they think embodies the features that make the ideal leader, regardless of their ethnicity or cultural background, they often mention Barack Obama. As you dig a little deeper into their reasons for this choice, we hear answers along the lines of: "he is authentic"; "he is so human"; "he seems to have such empathy"; "he is such an incredible motivator"; "he has the gift of credibility"; "he knows how to engage people in his story or project"; "I never have the feeling he wants to prove something or needs to know things better at all cost"; or "he seems to be immensely value-driven."

However, the reply that keeps coming back is: "He can admit when he has made a mistake."

Right after his election into office a few years ago, Obama proved that he owns up to his mistakes. The euphoria around his "Yes, We Can" campaign had hardly subsided when he had to face his responsibilities. He nominated a Treasury Secretary who, it emerged a few weeks later, appeared to have been involved in a corruption case. Many leaders and politicians would have pleaded "not guilty", claiming that they were unaware of the secretary's wrongdoings. Not so Obama. At a hastily arranged press conference, he chose to show he is vulnerable, openly admitting his mistake, taking full responsibility for it and announcing what he was going to do about it.

As a result, there was hardly any negative press; not one article questioned his integrity or expertise. Instead, he was praised for his openness, honesty and decisiveness. He was the leader that the world needed at the time.

Showing vulnerability is still difficult in today's corporate culture. What boss has the courage to admit that he simply does not know? In asking a question, you begin to answer it.

1. WHAT CAN COACHING ACHIEVE?

Coaching will not turn you into another person, but it will change the way you think about yourself as a person and as a manager. It is a mental change that you are setting in motion. Consequently, you evolve, you improve, and you change the way you function, causing a ripple effect: as you change, something happens to your environment—it changes along with you. Coaching sets this process of change in motion. Even if you are a good manager, even if you are satisfied with your life, your work, your company, perhaps you can do much better.

Self-improvement may not be what you had in mind. Most of us like to hold on to the status quo once we have figured out how to function at work and at home. Every change causes anxiety, discomfort and instability, every change requires a whole new quest.

You have the choice to take control of your life and explore ways to improve yourself. Choosing to live a more conscious life helps you become better equipped to deal with changes and unexpected blows. Like it or not, obstacles will appear in the process. No one escapes change.

Coaching is an efficient way to real self-improvement and to making choices that fit you and your situation. Coaching helps you to live more consciously by getting to know yourself better.

The Johari Window[2] (below) represents the different aspects of self-awareness. The four sections of the window represent the awareness we have of ourselves and the awareness others have of us.

	I look at myself	
Others look at me	The public self	The private [or hidden] self
	The unknown self	My blind spot

The Johari Window

You are aware of your private self and your public self. You know these sides to you. A coach, however, can teach you those parts still unknown to you: your unknown self (subconscious) and your blind spots.

The nature of blind spots is that you will not discover them on your own. Self-coaching is impossible in this context; hence the need for an external coach.

You gain insights into yourself from your coach's feedback, which enables you to reduce your blind spots and helps you understand better the effect you have on others. You become familiar with the unconscious thoughts and beliefs that drive your behaviour, and you learn how you can influence them to arrive at a different set of behaviours. Better self-knowledge leads to greater self-confidence and greater self-confidence helps you deal better with change.

The world keeps turning around - Corporate Life version 2.0
The way we typically handle rapid changes in companies is through a directive management style. In the process we fail to take advantage of the available potential of all employees. Instead we use control and reporting until we drown in it.

How can we become smarter in motivating people? Can we do this in a more human way?

The new paradigm is beginning to place values such as happiness, community, cooperation and sustainability in the foreground. Coaching is a way to support the transition from the old to the new paradigm. If we presume that *potential* is becoming the new currency, we need to expand our perception–through coaching–to ensure that we actually benefit from all that potential.

Paradigm shift

OUTGOING PARADIGMS

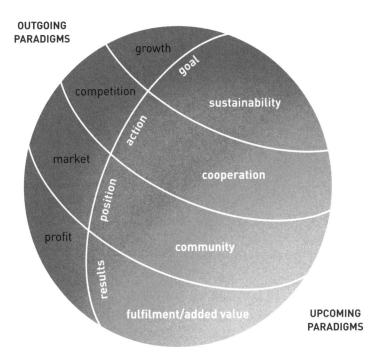

growth

goal

competition

sustainability

action

market

cooperation

position

profit

community

results

fulfilment/added value

UPCOMING PARADIGMS

KRISTINA MAES
– GLOBAL SALES MANAGER TERUMO EUROPE N.V.

I requested coaching because traditional training courses did not provide me with the solutions I needed to enable the new department in our company to function optimally.

It is the best gift a company can give you, especially if you know in advance where your sticking points lie and in which areas you need help.

Right from the intake conversation I knew that the coach was right for me and that we would work well together. After the first session, I came away with a number of insights and useful work methods/information.

The coach holds up a mirror to you. Through insistent questioning and allowing you to think about your own solutions and be your own guide, you gain awareness. You start to see where you have taken the wrong approach and how you could do it better. A coach can then suggest useful models based on his experience, which help you progress further. You continue to build upon each session in a constructive manner.

You get out of coaching what you put in. In other words, you must really want to be coached and put into practice your newly acquired knowledge and insights. If you are committed to do so, there is no substitute for coaching.

2

A coach?
Not for me,
thanks!

PART 2

A COACH? NOT FOR ME, THANKS!

While there has been more openness towards coaching in recent years, most managers still hesitate to take the step of hiring a coach for themselves. We see all kinds of prejudices, negative beliefs and denial about the need for a coach.

We frequently hear statements such as, "I am getting results. Why would I need a coach?" or "They must think I am good if they made me a manager. I have made it this far without a coach, so ..." or "I don't need a coach. I am coaching myself."

In the following chapter, we will address a few common questions to give you a better understanding of the essence of coaching, the most common coaching topics, what coaches do, and more.

I. PREJUDICES AGAINST COACHING

1. COACHING IS FOR PEOPLE WITH PROBLEMS. I DON'T HAVE ANY PROBLEMS

Unfortunately coaches are often called in only when problems or difficult situations arise. For example, a coach will be hired when employees no longer function according to expectations—such as when a manager scores low in the area of people management during an assessment.

Coaches are also typically requested when a team no longer functions as it should or when a situation has got out of kilter. Here coaching has a *reactive* function. This is still the most common scenario today, and with good reason: coaches can provide relief in these situations.

If coaching is seen as a reactive strategy only, it follows that you should not ask for a coach if you don't have problems. Who knows, a coach might even create problems! A coach makes you aware of all kinds of things that you have never (or hardly ever) thought about. Aspects that have always been taken for granted are now being questioned in the coaching process. In other words: coaching does not make things easier.

From reactive to proactive

Coaching can certainly offer solutions. However, the power of coaching goes much further. Coaching can also be used proactively. *Proactive coaching* does not focus on a problem; it looks towards creating opportunities.

Imagine that you have an important meeting coming up. Together with your coach you analyse what the meeting means for you. Through questioning, you and your coach explore various scenarios, the needs of the participants and their possible reactions leaving you well equipped to enter the meeting with confidence. Such an approach gives you energy, it stimulates you and inspires others.

A 10-minute coaching session for more courage

Chris is giving a presentation to a client this afternoon and is terribly apprehensive. Jan, his boss, notices Chris' qualms. He takes Chris aside and suggests a few minutes of coaching. Jan asks Chris a few questions, including: "What is it exactly that you are worried about?", "What do you fear might happen?", "What else could happen?", and "How can you look at the situation differently?"

Thanks to these questions, Chris manages to look at his presentation through different eyes. He is also able to see the more positive aspects of the pending presentation and thus overcome his trepidations.

Questions of this type give you the courage to face your battles. Looking at coaching from this perspective makes it less taboo. It lowers the threshold and allows companies to invite coaching to become part of everyday business activities.

Regret prevention

Proactive coaching helps you make more conscious choices, choices that are right for you. Coaching enables you to focus on what helps you, what you need to fully believe in your choices, your career and your life. Coaching also teaches you to prevent situations occurring that you might regret later.

In her book *The Top Five Regrets of the Dying*, Australian Bronnie Ware, lists the most frequent admissions of regret heard in her time working as a nurse in palliative care.

1. "I wish I'd had the courage to live a life true to myself, not the life others expected of me." When people approach the end of their lives, they are confronted with those dreams barely fulfilled or not at all. At that moment, they also understand that it was because of the choices they made.

2. "I wish I had not worked so hard." Patients often regretted putting too much time into their work and spending too little time with their children as they were growing up. They also felt they had failed to spend quality time with their partners.

3. "I wish I'd had the courage to express my feelings." Many had suppressed their feelings to keep the peace. As a result, they had settled for a mediocre existence, never becoming who they wanted to be. Many patients had developed illnesses relating to the bitterness and resentment they carried as a result.

4. "I wish I had stayed in touch with my friends." Often they did not realise the benefits of old friends until their dying weeks. There

were many deep regrets about not giving friendships the time and effort that they deserved. Everyone misses their friends when they are dying.

5. "I wish I had let myself be happier." According to Ware, this was a surprisingly common regret. Many patients did not realise until the end that happiness is a choice. They had remained stuck in old patterns and habits.

Questioning yourself from time to time can reduce regrets over chances not taken or choices not made. This is not to say self-reflection of this kind will necessarily make your life easier. Coaching is for those who dare and have the courage to question their lives, their behaviour, their fears and successes. It is for people who take responsibility and who have the resolve to dig deeper.

Often managers assume that there is nothing to work on because they are doing well. This can be the case—for the moment. Nevertheless, change is the only constant these days. Most people find themselves in a competitive work environment in which they have to deal with great complexity, rapid changes, and permanent job insecurity. The pressure is relentless. We are expected to perform at the highest levels, day in, day out. Slowing down is not an option for most and every misstep leads to delays and possible finger pointing. The fear of failure prevents us from living a life of passion guided by what motivates us from within.

The necessity for maintenance

Even if you are managing well, the need for improvement and fine-tuning never ends. Guided by previous experience, we discard what doesn't work and stick to what has brought us success. Yet this is how we continually narrow down our options over a lifetime. We often realise too late that the approaches we have used with success in the past may no longer be suitable. What works today, may not work tomorrow.

It is therefore important that we remain alert and motivated—or rather, that we do not become demotivated. This consumes a lot of energy. We all need to take charge of sustaining motivation ourselves, because our own managers are far too busy keeping *themselves* motivated. Every well-functioning machine needs maintenance— and so do we. Taking time for reflection about what motivates and demotivates us, about what works and what seems to suit us less, is our responsibility. Taking time for ourselves is, however, still taboo in our work contexts; it makes us look like we are stragglers. However, 'working smarter, not harder' means that we must take time every now and then to examine what motivates and drives us.

Inner motivation is created through a combination of related external factors (work context, working conditions, salary, colleagues, type of boss) and the feeling that we are doing what we are supposed to be doing with our lives and at work.

Motivation

In general, there are two ways people motivate themselves:

1) They are facing a difficult situation and would like to avoid it. Their motivation to change is fed by the desire to get away from something ('away from' motivation)
2) They have a vision, a dream, an ideal situation that attracts them. Their motivation is focused on the future ('towards' motivation).

When a promotion opportunity arises, do I choose to take the promotion because the new job fits me like a glove and/or do I choose to take the promotion primarily because I want to escape what I am doing today?

Awareness of what we want to go 'towards' and 'away from' sets us in motion. Thus, we only evolve when we feel that there is a conflict between our goal (or our expectations) and our current reality. As long as people don't perceive a personal challenge, they will continue to do what they have always done.

If you want change, you have to start by changing yourself. Your changes will tip the balance. As you change, your colleagues cannot remain unaffected. You are a mirror for them, which will provoke a reaction on their part.

When others change, we are often inspired to move along with them. We have the choice to either discourage them through ridicule, doubt their chances of success, or to be curious and explore what they have in mind and what kind of results they expect. Our reaction to change in others is also up to us.

> *Koen (35) participated in an NLP course that included a segment on personal coaching. According to Koen, the experience "opened his eyes". As a result of his insights, he has implemented a new kind of management in the workplace. More attention is paid to how things happen and there is greater understanding about what leads to success and what doesn't. There are more questions than instructions due to their understanding that everyone is different and has good intentions, even if the results are sometimes disappointing.*

> *Through reflection and mirroring, management has begun to understand why employees sometimes react the way they do, which has helped managers to deal with those reactions in a different manner. Instead of stamping out fires, they are seeking dialogue with their employees. These two-way conversations lead to greater mutual respect than impersonal instructions via email.*

Many organisations are stuck in a *blame culture*. Everything is a priority, everything is urgent —you are living on your wits. Stamping out fires seems to be a fact of company life. Can't stand the heat? Then get out of the kitchen. Simple. If you don't want to adapt your life to the high demands of an international job, you are not up for it, the saying goes.

Bosses claim that the employees are not cooperating; employees say the bosses are at fault. This is a well-known phenomenon that leads to inefficiency and stagnation—until you ask, "What is difficult about this?" "What prevents you from doing something about this situation?"

Through coaching, people learn to understand the causes and dynamics of those wild fires, as well as how they are contributing to them. Individuals become more aware of their place and role in the bigger picture. This creates greater understanding for each other and between the different levels. Addressing people about their personal impact, their areas of responsibility—*that* is where the power of coaching lies.

2. I HAVE PLENTY OF EXPERIENCE. WHAT CAN A COACH TEACH ME?

This misconception is rooted in the erroneous belief that a coach's role is to give advice. And if you have tons of experience, or are the expert in your field, how can a coach possibly teach you anything?

"I have been around so long. What do I need a coach for? I have all the experience in the world. A coach is not for me." As coaches, we come across this attitude regularly, in one form or another.

However, coaching is not about dispensing advice or answers. Coaching is about asking questions and challenging *you* to make meaningful choices. A coachee needs to find his own answers and solutions. It's not the coach, but the client who is the expert in his life and his way of functioning. All the answers he needs at any given moment lie within him. The coach's role is to bring these answers to the surface. A coach therefore helps by asking the right questions rather than by giving the right answers.

Our thoughts govern our behaviour. Many of us still have to come to grips with this idea. We look for explanations, excuses and pretexts to avoid doing something. And we are convinced that we do not have the power to change things.

And that's exactly where the coach comes in. What thoughts are standing in your way? What is it that prevents you from doing precisely what you need to be doing? A coach does not have that information. He is not an expert on your life—you are. You alone are at the wheel, but the coach can help you read the map.

3. I DON'T NEED COACHING. MANAGEMENT DOES

Many people consider their company to be the source of all problems and they talk as if issues have nothing to do with them, when in fact they are an integral part of the whole. All that troubles the company is blamed on its structure or culture, management's decisions, or the economic environment. Such a mindset leads to a lot of finger pointing. Line managers accuse the department manager, the department manager points at the CEO, and the CEO faults the banking crisis.

In uncertain times, this kind of blame game intensifies and we quickly begin to feel powerless. Employees often work as hard, if not harder, with fewer results than before the crisis. And you hear comments such as: "How can I perform at my best if the rest of the company is not doing its share?" or, "Working harder won't get us anywhere, just look how hard the crisis is hitting us."

Company structures can foster such attitudes. It is often hard for employees in decentralised matrix structures, who belong to various teams and report to various supervisors, to see their part in the greater picture. Such structures prevent them from seeing their personal involvement in the overall performance of the company. They have a small input in one project and a role in another; they belong partially to one department or to none at all. In the end, they do not get a sense of how important their personal contribution was to the process.

Employees often feel that they are being reduced to performing part of a process or simply carrying out a job description. Small wonder they have little interest in taking responsibility for seeking improvements or change. Change is not on their mind either if they are getting bogged down in endless workplace procedures. Ironically, the goal of ISO (International Organization for Standardization) certifications is to create greater quality control and more focus on objectives. However, the stringent directives in the (SOPs) Standard Operating Procedures invariably reduce people's interest in staying on the ball and seeking improvements. Of course, the solution lies somewhere in the middle. SOPs should not be considered an alibi for rote behaviour, but a basis for self-governance and common sense.

The reaction of people who are asked to receive coaching is often: "Do I need to change? I am doing my best to follow procedures. I am doing what's in my job description. Is there anything that I should do differently?" or, "*We* have to get coaching while management is the source of the malaise!"

This can reflect a deep-seated fear: the fear of failure; the fear of finding out that you might be part of the problem. Or, more positively: the fear of having to take responsibility for contributing to the solution.

This brings up an even greater and more fundamental fear: that your efforts may hardly matter. Employees are prepared, in theory, to look at themselves and see what they could change. However, often they prefer not to start the process because they don't believe that their personal development can make a difference in their work environment. The fundamental question here is perhaps: "Do you believe that coaching can help you bring about change in yourself and in your company?" If the answer is "yes" then the idea "I don't need to be coached—management does" has no foundations.

4. COACHING IS FOR TOP MANAGERS ONLY

Executive coaching or coaching of upper management appears to be making greater inroads in companies than coaching of lower level employees. The notion that CEOs or top managers are working with a coach to support them in making difficult decisions in complex situations is increasingly accepted.

When CEOs make well thought out and innovative decisions, it will inevitably affect the levels below. The newly expanded horizons of top managers lead to them having higher expectations of others. (It is hard to kick old habits)

Organisations change and their employees develop alongside this, their evolution is often based on a process of trial and error. We do things one way today and, if that does not work, differently next time. If we still don't have the results we want, we try something else the day after. This natural evolution is based on experimentation, without giving much thought to the deeper reasons for failures or errors. Organisations that are stuck in such *action-to-action patterns*, whether on a managerial or executive level (or both), have enormous difficulties with change of any kind. What follows is more stamping out of wild fires to solve the mistakes of the previous experiment.

CEOs who are being coached understand that there is more than one way to look at reality, and they challenge their employees to begin to explore as well. Companies that provide for coaching at all levels are more successful in managing change. They understand that not only top managers benefit from an exercise in reflection and that they can obtain higher commitment through coaching at lower and middle management. Commitment in a company makes a difference: it encourages leaders at all levels to come up with their own thoughts and to express their doubts and ideas.

Employees are often only too happy to complain about management and the way they are being managed. They accuse management of not having any vision and of only responding to crises. Managers in companies with a coaching mindset deal with such reactions in a more thoughtful manner. Stamping out fires is a fact of company life. Through coaching, though, you can show employees how they contribute to these fires and how they can help prevent them in the future.

Making the move from colleague to supervisor without losing face

A production company in Aarschot has been giving training called 'Leading with a Coaching Mindset' to all its first-time managers since 2002. Aligned with the motto 'workers with leadership potential rise up to become team leaders', the company provides its employees with five half-days of module-based training on leadership and coaching, spread out over a period. The new managers are monitored by an internal coach and an HR officer and supported to carry out their action plans, and apply on the work floor what they have learned during the training. The internal coach also discusses their progress, and any hurdles they might have experienced, with them.

Of course, it is not uncommon for employees to become supervisors of former colleagues. Many new managers are friends with their former colleagues. They took breaks together, at times longer than they were supposed to, and often joined forces against decisions from management. Now, the managers are faced with ensuring that their former buddies get back to work on time. If you, as a new manager, fail to handle this well, you will lose face and become isolated. Managing your former work buddies can be a source of conflict.

The most important question for a first-time manager is: How do I create a defined distance without becoming an adversary in the eyes of my former colleagues? How do I create distance or demand discipline and still remain involved?

There is no standard answer. Dilemmas of this nature are too complicated for new managers to solve on their own. To solve them requires reflection and awareness. Often, these new leaders decide not to really manage but to remain friends. However, this usually accomplishes little and it doesn't make management happy. Alternatively, the new leaders go in the opposite direction and become demanding and tyrannical, which makes their fear of losing their friends a self-fulfilling prophecy.

The company's CEO, a staunch supporter of the coaching project, swears that he knows exactly who followed the training and who didn't. He immediately notices the difference in the team leaders.

It's a numbers game

Coaching often starts with executive management. Top managers who have benefited from coaching are then likely to see the value of it for their employees and what it brings to the company. But how do we go about infusing middle and lower management with coaching?

Most companies opt to work with a combination of training and coaching. The theory behind coaching is usually taught in short group sessions and applied through exercises and on the work floor. One manager-coach, a buddy or an internal HR coach closely watches the trainees in action and gives them feedback in individual follow-up sessions. The training material becomes less abstract and the participants can get straight to work.

In the beginning, above all, the participants need information, which they receive during the training, as well as the follow-up talks with their coaches. The acquired knowledge needs to be translated and applied. The second part is at least as important as the first. This is how coaching can be spread throughout the whole organisation. What was initially reserved for management is made available to the whole company.

Formally establishing coaching sessions in the workplace also provides an acceptable alibi for workers to get away from the daily grind, where the attitude often prevails that to work means to be *doing something* as opposed to 'sitting around and contemplating', or that it is more important to be visibly busy than to think things through.

Making reflection a habit

The number of internal coaches is increasing rapidly as, in many companies, coaching brings with it the need for follow-up training sessions — and not only for managers. Everyone is looking to continually improve. Of course, coaching is not the only means to do so. Implementing quality training sessions also ensures time for personal reflection to translate new ideas into concrete action plans.

Putting aside time for training
Genencor offers a training module entitled, "Self-management and Communication with Impact" to its 100 employees. Everyone from the work floor to the executives receives seven half-days of training on self-leadership, as well as three hours of coaching. The goal is both to ensure that people work and communicate from an open state of mind, and to create an awareness of what is possible in leadership and communication. People become more conscious of their strengths and their weaknesses and actively develop their potential.

5. SUCCESSFUL MANAGERS DON'T NEED A COACH

Managers who measure their success by how high or well they have climbed the career ladder and the status they have achieved often believe that there is little they can still learn or that they no longer need support.

Georges Anthoon, 56

After having successfully held various HR director positions, Georges Anthoon (56) wrote a bestseller. He is sought after by the most important business schools. He exudes a professional image. What could a coach possibly do for him? Surely it is obvious that he knows what he is doing? If anything, he can teach others the path to success. Or is there more to coaching? Is there another way to look at coaching? More about that in Chapter 4.

As we saw in Chapter 1, it gets lonely at the top. Who dares to challenge successful people? The more successful you are, the less honest the feedback you get and the more flatterers you find at your door. How can you know whether someone is saying what you want to hear or whether he genuinely appreciates you? And those who keep their opposing opinions to themselves: are they not simply trying to impress you, to stay in your good graces?

Tony, 56, CFO

Tony (56) is a CEO and in charge of optimisation processes for financial procedures at an international level. He supervises internal auditors in different countries. He is highly successful in his field and is consulted by experts at several consulting firms.

However, a number of people in various countries don't follow his procedures, build their own variations. His solution: to use his persuasive powers to inform the hierarchy in the country, and to create sanctions should the rules not be followed. He then leaves the local auditors to their own devices. He feels that they have to live with the consequences. They had enough warning.

He refused to accept the advice of the local experts, who had told him from the beginning that their countries needed certain adaptations. Nobody ever held up a mirror to Tony or pointed out to him that the creation of, and implementation of a change platform happens primarily via human contact. The emails he received were cursory at best. The original topic of his coaching project was: "How can I impose an international strategy?" when in reality the issue was: "What can I do to increase commitment, despite cultural differences?"

Some perceive too much self-insight to be an obstacle to success. Why would you want to slow down and study the impact you have had? You have already proven that you are successful.

Nina (41), a bank manager, got to the top through sheer ambition. She wants to have everything under control. She is abrupt with her colleagues and afraid of change, because that means relinquishing control. In her early forties, she takes her first emotion-based decision and resolutely chooses love over her career. After one year, her relationship runs into problems, and she is emotionally shaken up. She goes to a one-off coaching session and thinks to herself, "That's enough." She runs away from herself. She does not have the courage to examine herself or her thinking patterns. She temporarily goes back to her old ways; i.e. chasing success by exerting control. It's the only way she knows. Those around her know only too well that she needs to change, but how does one approach someone with such a strong personality? What else needs to happen before she will look at her share of the problem?

Around the age of 45 to 50, we have moments when we look at the balance sheet of our lives. We ask fundamental questions such as: *Is this all there is? Have I been able to achieve all I wanted to achieve? What else do I want? Where are there still challenges for me? After you have achieved everything, after you have fought and won, after you have experienced wellbeing and wealth, what is the next step?* For many, these are difficult questions, which often reveal their own personal shortcomings.

Unfortunately, this is something we see a lot in CEOs. After having had so much success, they often experience a kind of emptiness inside. All their lives they measured themselves on external factors. Those who have a major impact in an organisation and those who give the impression that their private life is subordinate to their work life have not paid much attention to the common good. They do not see how important self-fulfilment is until they realise they do not have it.

Four coaches for Lukaku, the line trainers of Club Brugge and the psychologist …

He was called the greatest soccer talent of 2011. A dream transfer to Chelsea. Lukaku had such talent and yet, while based at Club Anderlecht, he had four coaches: one for technique; one for physical training, speed and agility; one for increasing the number of goals; and one for communicating with the press. Luxury? A waste of money? Not at all! A dire need!

It is not just individual athletes who have coaches. Teams also deploy a whole squad of specialised trainers to accompany them. Have you ever heard of the line trainers at Club Brugge? For each line (keepers, defense, midfield and offense) they use dedicated trainer-coaches.

The bottom line is: having talent is no longer enough in today's soccer world. The same applies to the business world. Companies, too, need to spot talent and develop it to the fullest. They also need to include classic training, which works on competencies, behaviour and values.

There is another phenomenon evident in today's sports world. Many top athletes choose to add an external (mental) coach to their existing coaching teams. To be sure, some soccer players have the tendency to belittle their "shrink". Nevertheless, there are a number of examples of teams and top athletes who seek psychological guidance. Athletes may wrestle with their confidence or have been thrown out of balance due to personal issues. Sometimes teams are no longer prepared to go through the fire for their trainers and/or their team mates, which leads to a drop in their athletic performance.

This is when the role of the external coach becomes crucial. He can open eyes, restore trust and improve team spirit. 'The body follows the mind,' is the motto. When your head is in a good state, athletic results can improve.

II. SHAPING THE FUTURE

> *"Don't think outside the box ... rather make sure you never get in the box!"*

1. WHY GO THROUGH ALL THAT TROUBLE?

"Everything passes. Most problems resolve themselves if I wait long enough. With a bit of luck, things will turn out in my favour."

If that is how you choose to think, you have a 50% chance that it will happen that way. You are assuming that your success is fuelled by external sources. And if it doesn't work out, you expect that you will be strong enough to deal with the consequences.

An alternative approach would be to try shaping your own luck and chances. A key principle in coaching is 'What you give attention to, grows'. We know from quantum physics that our thoughts influence reality. Why, then, would you *not* choose to shape your future?

Can you allow yourself to glow with happiness?
Can you allow yourself to experience joy?
Can you allow yourself to develop your talents?

Can you allow yourself to be yourself, exactly the way you are—unleashed?

These questions hold up a mirror for many of us. The kinds of (well-known) arguments that stand in the way include:

> We should not be overly happy, because it won't last long.
> We should not enjoy things too much, because that would be selfish.
> We should not try to be special, because then we could lose our friends.

These are some of the mechanisms that keep us small and humble. Can we really afford not to live life to the fullest? Many of us live on a limited bandwidth: not too many highs, not too many lows … because, if you take risks or make an effort, you could be disappointed. Avoiding taking risks appears to prevent failure—until you look back at your life and realise that you have always lived below your potential. Now, how is that for a definition of failure?

This potential to shape the future also applies to our private lives. Who says that a beautiful relationship, a great family and a fantastic job have to be mutually exclusive? Everyone can, in agreement with their partner, find ways to reap the benefits on all levels.

As coaches, we believe that you can shape your future. It is what we are doing and experiencing ourselves. The courage to look at all the subconscious constraints that keep you from making the most of your life and potential can make a big difference to your level of happiness.

2. WE ALL NEED TO LIVE WITH OUR STRENGTHS AND WEAKNESSES

We all compare ourselves to others on some level. The school system, as well as various assessment tools, helps us identify our strengths and weaknesses and we try to play to the former. Then someone who we consider no better than us gets a promotion or a more positive performance evaluation. We become angry at the supervisor, who obviously was not able to sufficiently recognise our qualities, or paralysed by the thought that we are in some way inferior.

Anne, a consultant

Anne, a consultant, has the same diploma and the same competencies as one of her colleagues. When it comes to invoicing, however, the company bills a higher rate for the colleague. Anne is having a hard time dealing with this and sees it as unjustified discrimination. She sends an angry mail to her boss ... What does her colleague have that she doesn't?

Such reactions are a form of self-protection. Shooting the messenger, in this case the boss, is a protection mechanism—a way to avoid looking at our own shortcomings, to avoid having to take responsibility. Often, this kind of response leads to a serious deterioration of the relationship with our supervisor.

The notion that someone might have become better than us and is compensated accordingly is difficult to swallow. Many of us find it difficult to accept that there are various factors at play. We have trouble making distinctions between these factors.

The issue is not just differences in competencies. Harnessing success is also about the way we show ourselves to others, the way we communicate about what we are good at, and our resilience in the face of setbacks. We are usually highly motivated when it comes to proving that we are equally competent and, in the short term, this can make a difference. In the long run, however, we must learn to believe more in ourselves and feel confident enough to show our talents, our strengths and who we really are.

A coach will explore with you what is preventing you from showing what you have to offer, as well as what you need to do to show your strengths. You can explore on your own, of course, but chances are that you will run around in circles.

3. COACHING IS ONLY ABOUT FUNCTIONING PROFESSIONALLY

How do you function at work and beyond? Are you different at work than in your private life? Do you have a professional persona and a non-professional one? And if you were to get coaching, which persona would you show: the professional one or the other?

No matter how much we like to tell ourselves that we function differently professionally, in essence we are the same person. Why then do we hide behind our professional persona? Is being professional a pretext for not getting in touch with our feelings? We are often being "professional" when we consider something not good enough. It has nothing to do with who you really are.

Everyone has thoughts, feelings and aspirations. You may not have shared your goals or vision. And why should you? You run the risk that others might belittle your ideas and consider you less competent. So you keep up the façade; act as if you are someone else at work. In coaching, it is really not helpful to keep up appearances. If you are pretending to yourself and to your coach, you will not get results. By pretending, you waste time, energy and money.

Keeping up appearances

Here is the bad news: To grow you must have the courage to face up to your uncomfortable truths, to look at the skeletons in your closet. As long as you don't know the underlying mechanisms that block you, as long as you don't know how you function or how your thoughts drive your behaviour, you are only fooling yourself. In coaching, you might as well lay bare your thoughts. If you don't, a good coach will quickly see through you.

Here is the good news: Coaches are bound by professional ethics. Confidentiality is an imperative in the coaching profession, and stipulated in the deontological code of the International Coaching Federation (ICF). Coaching is impossible without a base of trust between coach and coachee. The safety of a coaching relationship offers you a unique opportunity to grow. Imagine what a relief it will be to express your thoughts and feelings without censorship rather than hiding under a thick veneer of 'professionalism'.

4. A HOLIDAY OR A GOOD TALK WITH A FRIEND ALSO RELIEVE FRUSTRATION

Going on holiday is a wonderful way to relax; a holiday is an escape from frustration and tensions at work. During our holiday, we replace tension with relaxation. However, the effect of a holiday is usually short-lived, a sticking plaster for our frustrations. (Some say the effect is gone after three days of being back at work.) We can learn from holidays. With a coach, you can explore how to experience relaxation at work, without diminishing your performance.

A heart-to-heart with a friend can definitely provide relief—and it is cheaper than a coach! A *good* friend does not hold back honest feedback; he confronts you with your behaviour. He can challenge you. Moments like this are invaluable in our search for happiness and balance in life.

A coach is essentially a good friend who goes a step further and challenges you to make concrete plans of action. A coach does not back off after the first "yes, but." He has learned techniques that support you in overcoming your mental obstacles and in making your well thought-out decisions. He follows up with you, like a friendly watchdog, and looks for ways to dispel your doubts.

5. WORKING HOURS ARE FOR WORKING, NOT FOR "FEEL GOOD STUFF"

> *"The status quo is good enough. I do my best, and my problems are the same as everyone else's. In fact, my problems are really luxury problems. I have a roof over my head, bread on the table. I have work (that I like) and friends I can trust. What more could I want?"*

Often we placate ourselves to avoid having to make an extra effort, to stay away from introspection and uncomfortable feelings. We function relatively well, because we shut out our feelings. We have found ways to rationalise them. We steer our lives with our head and our body and heart must merely follow. It works well. We get results—until a crisis strikes.

Leen (52)

I always considered myself a professional who did everything to deliver the best service. I had no insurmountable problems. 'Where there is a will, there is a way ... giving up is not an option.' Those were my mottos. I did feel exhausted at times— that I had overstepped my limits—but I did not listen to my body. I became a slave to myself. There were various warning signs, such as chronic sinusitis and bouts of bronchitis, as well as several operations due to accidents from being too impulsive. But, people get better and recuperate—so, no problem, I thought. All I needed to do was to slow down a little and then carry on.

Then my body decided that it was time for me to listen and that I urgently needed to take a break. I suffered from burn-out. I was unable to do anything. I could no longer organise my thoughts or stand noise or light. My balance was off. All I could do was sleep. During my eight months of recuperation, I regained my pluck. I combined all kinds of therapies and body work, adjusted my diet, got massages, and slowly began doing sports again. I 'fought' my way through the burn-out by filling every minute in a meaningful way.

Coaching made me aware that I acted no differently during my 'recovery' than I did before my burn-out. 'Giving up' was still not in my vocabulary. I realised that my burn-out had a lot to do with my wanting to do everything perfectly. During my coaching sessions, I gained some valuable insights: I realised that I was so tired because I had suppressed the feeling of being tired; because I wanted to be able to do everything by myself; and because I wanted to please everyone. By working on these patterns, I gradually allowed myself to listen to my body and to set boundaries in a respectful manner.

Burn-out, depression, raised blood pressure, physical exhaustion …
all these are illnesses of today's hard-working men and women. In
essence, all are driven by one thought: *Am I good enough?*

What are our sources of self-esteem?
Comments from others? The ideal image of ourselves? Compari-
sons with our idols? We all seek the answer to the question, "When
will I be good enough?" Contemporary society and its high demands
are doing their share to make things worse.

There might have been a time when taking good care of yourself and
taking enough time for your family made you feel happy with yourself. You considered yourself a good father when you were making
enough money to take care of your family. You considered yourself a
good mother when you were giving your children what they needed
and when they were well disciplined. Our self-image today though is
increasingly subject to the societal dictum that we have to have accomplished something special or made an important contribution.
This shift leads to tension.

Becoming a good person requires reflection and slowing down; quiet time and self-observation; patience. Exploring, forgiving yourself
for earlier follies, all this does not happen overnight. It takes a long
journey of gaining awareness, of falling down and getting up, of many
uncomfortable questions that you may not want to answer because
you are stuck in self-judgement. A meaningful coaching process will
give you more self-esteem, a greater inner peace, which in turn will
also affect the people around you. This is change at a deeper level.

Do you have the courage to see who you really are?

If you really want to know who you are and what effect you have on other people, you need the courage to question yourself. You need to evolve to a higher level and unless you are aware that you need to evolve; it is not going to happen. That's the problem with the *blind spot syndrome*. Unless someone challenges you, or holds a mirror up to you, how you can discover your hidden potential and how you can find out about opportunities and options to really change your life.

III. THE ADDED VALUE OF COACHING

We try to keep up with the pace of our colleagues, or do better. Competitiveness and automation have created a world that requires us to act at nearly inhuman speed. We send an email and expect an answer within 24 hours. A voicemail or a text message should be replied to within the hour. We have forgotten that it does not *have* to be that way. The generation born after 1990 is doing things differently. These young people consciously choose to alternate between work time and private time. They are less a slave to themselves than the older generation, who cling to the belief that "working hard is noble."

A coach can help you arrange your priorities before your body decides for you.

1. WHAT CAN A COACH DO THAT I CAN'T?

A coach does not take part in your life or your work, and can therefore ask questions from an objective point of view. A coach has no stake in the outcome. You have the biggest stake and should therefore be encouraged by your coach to find an answer that comes close to what you really want.

A coach is skilled at listening to the key words that reveal your talents and values. They ask questions that lead to open, spontaneous answers. A coach cannot change the outcome, but he can help you see reality from a different perspective. He can help you find a perspective that is more useful to you at that particular moment. This will allow you to discover different options, to have more choices, to celebrate the decisions that *you* have made.

2. ALL THIS SLOWING DOWN! CHANGE MUST HAPPEN QUICKLY

Coaching only works if you make sure you turn your decisions into action. Simply following a workshop will not solve your problems. The process of becoming a manager and/or coach takes time; it is not merely about acquiring skills, but is about setting in motion a change in attitude that is based on your convictions and overcoming your subconscious fears.

3. A BOOK WILL TEACH ME JUST AS MUCH

Reading books is a good start and leads to growing awareness. A book can provide you with a number of new insights and perspectives, but it won't allow you to experience them. Knowledge gleaned from books is only effective if you *apply* it. Moreover, it is often hard to teach yourself. However, books don't have what it takes to give you a completely new perspective, because reality does not necessarily conform to its depiction in books. Books can help sharpen our ability to reflect. Books can contribute to our development, and yet they do not have the power to bring about effective change in behaviour. Not even this book. The only way to experience the true effect of coaching is to actually go through it.

4. COACHING IS SOFT AND INTANGIBLE. IT WON'T WORK

Performance management is often considered the "hard" part of management, while coaching is still regarded as a "soft" skill. However, coaching also has a hard aspect to it: coaching is not only about supporting the coachee, but also about questioning and urging action. Coaching can probably best be illustrated by comparing it with parenting. As a parent it is important to lend an attentive ear and to support and help your child without passing judgement. It is as important, however, to set limits and to be a critical sounding board. Similarly, coaches listen without judgement, but also act as a critical sounding board and push for action.

Coaching itself may not be tangible, but its results are both visible and palpable.

> The CEO of a large consulting company had this to say about employees who have undergone coaching: "I can always tell if people have had coaching. We never have to ask them: 'What is this going to bring you?' They see possibilities, show more enthusiasm and transform themselves. You have to believe that coaching will do something for you, and then the effect will be greater."

5. CHOOSING A COACH

If this book has made you curious about coaching, the following criteria can help you select a coach. A good coach is someone who:

> maintains a balance between listening and talking
> has the energy to set you in motion
> can tell you something about himself that you find intriguing

> makes you feel safe enough to place your trust in him
> is understanding but also challenges you
> has undergone a learning process himself
> has also made choices—consciously
> has been, and still is being, coached
> can hold up a mirror to you without claiming to know the truth
> understands that change is not easy
> is not patronising
> can stay objective

Selection criteria: A survey

In 'More Process, Less Insight. Survey Report: Trends in Executive Coach Selection' (2010), a study involving 40 major buying companies and about 300 coaches, Carol Braddick examines the criteria involved in selecting a coach, both from the buyers' points of view and that of the coaches. It is interesting to note that the coaches themselves assumed that their selection criteria were different from those of the buyers.

Buyers considered business experience more important than qualifications, while coaches reasoned the opposite. This can be partly explained by the different view each group holds of coaching. Coaches are essentially experts in *accompanying learning processes*. You don't have to have been a manager to be able to do that, but many managers are still of the belief that it is impossible to be guided by a coach efficiently without this coach having been, or being, an expert in their field. This makes sense in that the most important parameters managers use to assess an employee, are their career steps and business experience. Buyers are also convinced that they risk tarnishing *their* image if they present coaches without business or management experience to their company.

In addition, coaches often underestimate the importance of coaching models and coaching approaches to clients. Managers consider coaching models a tool, a tangible way to see whether they like a certain approach or not.

In the jungle of various qualifications held by coaches, it is difficult to compare them. For coaches who have really invested in themselves, it is only natural that qualification becomes an important factor; it is closely linked with their overall approach and vision of coaching.

Coaches look at whether there is a 'click' between coach and coachee, a kind of chemistry because it is a tremendous asset to growth to be able to reflect and act in an uninhibited and spontaneous way in a coaching process. Buyers seem to be less focused on this aspect –, an indication of their result orientation versus the process orientation of a coach.

Key criteria for selecting a coach

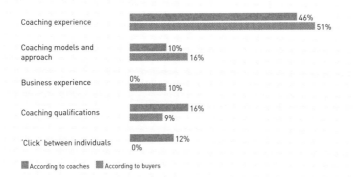

Coaching experience — 46% / 51%

Coaching models and approach — 10% / 16%

Business experience — 0% / 10%

Coaching qualifications — 16% / 9%

'Click' between individuals — 12% / 0%

According to coaches ■ According to buyers

Word of mouth remains the most effective way to find a coach. Testimonials from clients—that coaching works and that the cooperation went smoothly—are a coach's trump card.

Braddick's study also shows that both buyers and coaches have noticed a shift in how coaches are being selected. The market seems increasingly aware of what professional coaching means and the fact that some who call themselves coaches are really consultants or individual trainers. Furthermore, the selection processes of large companies via public tender often constitute a heavy administrative burden for coaches. This process also does not validate their coaching mindset, or essence.

Another trend in the field is the emergence of 'coach brokers', organisations that assist companies in finding a suitable coach. Large consultancy firms that have established credibility in other HR services are also calling on a group of associated freelancers. In addition, assessment centres for coaches are occasionally used. However, this is double work, because coaches who have been accredited by recognised organisations have already undergone an assessment process.

Many feel it is time to create a regulatory authority that lays down clear qualification criteria for coaches. Clients too are becoming aware of the importance of clear information on how coaches are trained and accredited.

What buyers value when selecting a coach		
Perception of buyers	Essential	Nice to have
1. Personal references or recommendations	53	45
2. Business experience	53	38
3. Coaching models and approach	48	40
4. Supervision by a qualified supervisor	40	35
5. Evidence of continued training	35	45
6. Qualification by a coaching institute	33	55
7. Accreditation by a school or professional organisation	33	53
8. Leadership in a professional organisation	36	51
9. Knowing coach personally	25	55
10. Contributions to coaching studies or the development of the profession	5	53

6. POINT OF DEPARTURE FOR COACHING

People who receive coaching because they are considered a "problem case", or because it is unclear whether they should be kept on at the company, are usually not terribly eager to be coached. However, where coaching is positioned as an instrument to assist talented employees (i.e. high potentials), it may be associated with status and success. Indeed, it would be ideal if, in the future, professional coaching was included in salary packages.

Some companies use internal coaches to accompany their executives. However, internal coaches can run into conflicts of interest due to the confidential information revealed during coaching conversations. In such cases, a clear contract needs to be established which states that even the internal coach's direct line manager needs to refrain from asking revealing questions about the coachee.

Since internal coaches are often HR business partners, they tend to wear at least two hats. In their role as HR managers, they primarily provide answers. As coaches they mainly ask questions. This dual role can lead to confusion and suspicion. A clear definition of roles—and communication thereof—to the line managers is therefore indispensable. Failing to do so will require each of them to continuously set boundaries themselves, which often leads to misunderstandings.

7. RETURN ON INVESTMENT

Changes in behaviour or actions, and leveraging of competencies inevitably have an impact on a company's results. It is only natural that changes in behaviour or convictions have an effect on individuals in the immediate environment. Whether, or to what extent, actions by top management, shifts in the market or moments of crises play a role is of course hard to determine.

In a study by McGovern et al, 100 clients mentioned the following effects of coaching:

Tangible effects of coaching

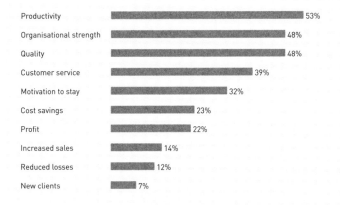

Productivity	53%
Organisational strength	48%
Quality	48%
Customer service	39%
Motivation to stay	32%
Cost savings	23%
Profit	22%
Increased sales	14%
Reduced losses	12%
New clients	7%

Intangible effects of coaching

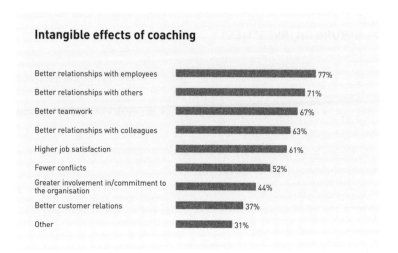

Better relationships with employees	77%
Better relationships with others	71%
Better teamwork	67%
Better relationships with colleagues	63%
Higher job satisfaction	61%
Fewer conflicts	52%
Greater involvement in/commitment to the organisation	44%
Better customer relations	37%
Other	31%

Subjective effect

The desire to make the effects of coaching measurable naturally stems from the focus on *results* in organisations. In their selection process, buyers try, above all, to exclude as many factors as possible that could lead to failure.

However, coaching is a form of intervention that can never be 100% controlled. The process is both well ordered (with structures and boundaries) and unpredictable, just like any other investment in development. The effects of coaching can never be measured fully, because each measure is based on personal and subjective perceptions.

In addition, the long-term effects of coaching are, to a large degree, mental and emotional. The manner in which someone considers and approaches things differently will manifest itself in his actions, both in his private and professional life. Still, it is of course difficult to measure the overall effect of coaching.

Nevertheless, if we ask coachees what they have perceived as a benefit of their coaching process, we get the following answers:

Subjective benefits according to coachees

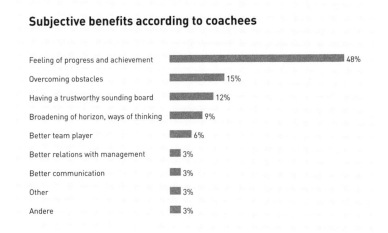

A feeling of achievement contributes to an improved attitude and self-image. Many employees rarely receive constructive feedback, or they are overly demanding of themselves and thus never satisfied. A lack of daily joy or satisfaction with yourself contributes to feeling blue, stressed and, in the long run, demotivated. Of course, happy employees are also more likely to attract customers.

Internal follow-up: key to success

Having someone follow up on our progress serves as a tremendous incentive to give our best and persevere when things get tough. The benefits of coaching are optimised when the coaching project is integrated into an internal follow-up process.

The direct supervisor assists in the beginning to help define the coaching objectives. It is essential for the manager and the coachee to have a joint discussion about the common goal and the expected outcome.

Neurological studies have shown that being able to share new insights immediately after acquiring them is essential for deepening and strengthening new neural pathways in the brain. A newly gained perspective is always delicate and can quickly fade away without immediate expression. A manager's interest in the progress of the coachee can be highly motivating, provided he does so in a predominantly appreciative manner, with plenty of behavioural tips. Of course, it is always up to the coachee whether and to what extent, he wants to entrust his manager (or HR) with what is being discussed in the coaching sessions.

8. COACHING AS A WAY OF LIFE

Managers increasingly realise the importance of playing a more holistic role of *manager-coach*. Yet lack of knowledge and insecurity may prevent them from embracing that role. They often wonder - *what exactly does a coach do?* The hidden thought behind that question is: *What can a coach do that I can't? What knowledge does a coach have that I don't?*

Coaching, however, is not about knowledge or science, it is a way of life. Coaching is the result of reflection; it is the art of observation. It is about where you stand in life, how you look at people and events and how you deal with them. One person may have more of a natural aptitude for this approach than another. The good news is that anyone who is prepared to learn can coach. The first step is to develop proper attention skills for the other person.

Career-long coaching

Imagine you are a 24-year-old (recently graduated)
marketing employee and you are given an assistant: your first
management role. Imagine that you are offered coaching to
support you in this role. Thanks to the coaching you receive,
you immediately apply what you are learning in a leadership
course. You overcome your personal obstacles more easily.
You have a more conscious leadership experience and you
recognise the difference cooperation can make. Young people
are, in general, much more open for establishing new patterns.
Thus, if you get off to a good start, you can immediately and
consciously develop better leadership patterns. As a young
executive there is very little you have to unlearn.

Three years later, you get a second promotion, becoming
business marketing manager with one junior and two senior
employees under you. You are offered a coaching programme,
this time to develop your strategic skills. You have a tendency
to go back to an operational mode—planning, organising,
checking, controlling—because that is what you were
rewarded for in the past. In your new role you have to learn
how to move away from that approach, to look for trends, and
to carefully watch the market. This is challenging, because you
are constantly being pulled back to your operational ways of
the past.

Another three years later (you are now 30), you are being
prepped to become the marketing director. This time you are
offered coaching to help you learn how to stay away from
certain issues, take a broader perspective and avoid being
dragged into micro-problems (because these are being
handled by others). You examine your thoughts as you are
confronted with new challenges. Over the years, you have
learned to handle change more smoothly. You don't resist

being guided by a coach, because you are used to it. Indeed, coaching is part of your salary package; it is your right.

If a company includes coaching in its salary package to help an employee to develop himself or if a recruitment agency offers coaching to help a newcomer make a smooth transition, would that be considered extravagant?

In many companies, new employees are under tremendous pressure. Certainly managers are too. Providing a coach for support creates a win-win situation; both firm and individual benefit. It is an illusion that people can cope with such speed, complexity and high demands without regularly taking some distance from the job and making conscious choices.

9. WHAT IF COACHING BECAME MANDATORY FOR EVERY MANAGER?

Perhaps that is the direction in which we are going: it will become a matter, of course, that managers are coached throughout their careers and perhaps become coaches themselves.

A CEO also needs someone who challenges him to evolve to the next level. As more executives are being coached, we achieve a larger critical mass of additional coaches. They certainly become aware of the added value of coaching. That is how we establish a tool for sustainable growth: by paying more attention to results *and* to people. Organisations are a critical part of our society. More coaching creates greater sustainability in our society.

10. THE ADDED VALUE OF A COACHING CERTIFICATE

It goes without saying that a coaching certificate is no absolute guarantee for a good coaching service, just as a medical diploma is no guarantee for correct diagnosis or medical treatment.

A survey by *Harvard Business Review* showed that a few more respondents thought it important for a coach to have a certificate. By contrast, only one in 2.23 persons found that psychological training was important.

A coaching study undertaken by the International Coaching Federation (ICF) reveals that 78% of the 12,133 coaches interviewed believed that a certificate should be required. The ICF certificate does offer the guarantee that a coach agrees to abide by the ethical and professional code of conduct, which states how important it is to distinguish coaching from other professions.

Every now and then a coach is refused his certificate because he has not (yet) acquired the proper coaching attitude. A certificate can therefore assure the client that the coach knows what it takes, because he has been thoroughly screened according to professional standards. Whether the coach later applies those standards is, of course, up to him.

When choosing a coach, we suggest asking how many hours per year of continued education he is planning to take to increase his level of professionalism. This serves as proof as to how open a coach is to change—a key quality of a good coach.

LUC VAN HERCK
– CEO BOFROST BELGIUM

What if someone refuses to be coached?

I used to be convinced that my way of thinking, the way I acted, my approach, my feelings, my perspective of the world and everyone who lived in it, were correct.

But when, years later, I became involved in a relationship with a charming woman, I realised that there were definitely some differences between her and me. At work I am the general director of a company with about 500 employees. I am 48 years old, and there is quite a big difference between me and the younger generation in both the ways we think and act.

As a result, I decided I had to do something to develop my performance at work to a level satisfactory to my staff, my supervisors and myself, as well as to preserve my relationship.

I had heard a lot about coaching and I signed up for training to become a personal coach and finally understand what it all means. However, because of my busy agenda at work, and possibly because of my own resistance, I quickly dropped out of the programme. My excuse: I have too much pressure in my life to really take the time to think.

Nonetheless, I understood that I had to get rid of my bias against new things and began with an individual coaching programme.

By taking this step, I learned more about myself, but above all, I learned how my behaviour, my way of thinking, judgements or prejudices affected other people. It was a confirmation of what my wife and some employees had already told me over the years. Through coaching, it became crystal clear that if I wanted to be happier, I had to start with myself.

Did I become another person through coaching? I think I have become someone who has more understanding for others, who can let others be who they are. I am able to be myself today without wanting others to change in my direction.

Individual coaching sessions gave me insight into my rigid thinking, as well as a lesson in humility and respect towards others, and this has made me a happier person.

3

Coaching:
Do you dare?

PART 3

COACHING: DO YOU DARE?

Coaching is still considered somewhat of a taboo in the business world. If you, as a manager, hire a coach you may worry about being judged incompetent should the news get out. However, once you have taken that first step, you will see that this is not the case.

Being coached requires courage and determination. It is important to be able to question yourself; to see your own blind spots; to step out of your comfort zone; to take responsibility. You need to have the desire and courage to reflect on yourself and continue to be an agent of change for others.

I. FEARS THAT HOLD US BACK

To find out what keeps us from moving forward, let's have a look at the seven basic fears as described by Napoleon Hill[4]:

a. **The fear of criticism: "what will they think or say about me?"**
   Rejection can certainly leave a dent in our self-confidence. Can we allow ourselves to be the way we are? For many adults this is an issue they (subconsciously) grapple with at various times in their lives. The quest for our personal identity is a lifelong process.

b. **The fear of poverty, of losing what we have**
   Losing what we have, especially if it costs us a tremendous effort to acquire it, feels like personal failure. If we tie our self-image to financial and material results—which we can also lose—then it does indeed feel like going back to square one. However, the fact is that we are a lot more than the sum of our material possessions.

c. **The fear of physical pain and illness**
   Physical pain or illnesses are limiting our freedom, our quality of life. At least that is what it appears to be. But people who are paralysed and/or live with another handicap prove that they can also be happy. It depends on what you focus on.

d. The fear of aging, of losing one's youth, of decline

Youth is not a question of physical state but a way of looking from the inside out. As Sammy Davis Jr. said: "It is never too late for a happy youth."

e. The fear of not being loved (anymore)

Or the fear of being rejected or left behind. Or the fear of not being considered nice. It means that you live from one compromise to another and it makes it harder for others to see who you really are.

f. The fear of losing our freedom

That is why being locked up in a small cell is considered such a punishment. However, what most people don't understand is that as a result of the sheer fear of losing something, they are constructing an invisible wall around themselves. The only real freedom is to choose life in its entirety, even if it is scary.

g. The fear of death

This fear seems to be the grandfather of all fears. The fear of having lived a life that has contributed little, of not having been useful. Paradoxically, it is the fear of death that prevents us from living life to the fullest.

When looking through eyes of fear during coaching, we find the following variations:

1. Fear of change
2. Fear of the mirror of success and perfection
3. Fear of your less attractive or dark sides
4. Fear that others might stand in the way of your success
5. Fear of getting to know yourself
6. Fear of abuse of trust

7. Fear of discovering all your talents
8. Fear of allowing yourself to be happy
9. Fear of becoming a different person
10. Fear of losing self-confidence
11. Fear of confronting your self-saboteur

Challenge yourself by asking to what extent these fears or concerns around being coached play a role in your life:

- *I will become a different person and I could lose all my parameters and acquired comforts;*
- *People might consider me 'special' and accept me less;*
- *I will show my vulnerabilities and people might take advantage of me;*
- *I will feel small when presented with a mirror of success and perfection;*
- *I will have to confront my less attractive sides;*
- *I will realise how I continuously sabotage my growth and my happiness;*
- *I will understand that there are many talents that I am not tapping into;*
- *I will realise that the choices I have made were not my choices. I will have to take responsibility for this; I will have to make big decisions;*
- *I will have to anticipate conflicts with others to achieve my own personal success;*
- *I will feel more content and happier while others are not (yet).*

In the rest of this chapter we will reflect on each of these fears.

1. FEAR OF CHANGE

Although coaching is becoming more mainstream, many executives still shy away from it. Much of this reaction has to do with fear and shame: *What will the coach do with me? What will the effect of coaching be on me— and on my work environment? What will they think of me if I need a coach?* Fear of change sometimes goes even deeper: *What will the effect of business coaching be on my private life? If I change, what will that do to my partner?*

The latter fear is based on the assumption that, if you evolve and change, you might lose your partner. In some cases, when the partner does not evolve together with the coachee, this can lead to problems.

Eveline (35)

Eveline is a caring woman, always there for her husband, her children and her colleagues. She gets satisfaction from serving others. It gives meaning to her life. She also has a tendency to be attracted to men with a dominant streak. Strong men give her a sense of security, a feeling of safety.
At work, Eveline was told that she should set boundaries more often, become more assertive. She understood how this could benefit her, but continued to feel overwhelmed with work, never daring to say no. She was going beyond her limits and under a lot of stress, which she took home with her.

In her coaching sessions we worked on the basic emotions that fuel her need to serve. We also discussed her concern that others might feel let down and that she might come across as selfish if she doesn't do what others ask of her.

The changes in her behaviour as a result of her coaching
manifested themselves at work, but also at home. Eveline
slowly but surely began to take time for herself. She went to
gym instead of ironing three times a week. She also began to
speak her mind. This was new to her husband, who was used
to her doing whatever he told her to do. Fortunately, her coach
made sure that Eveline could gradually involve her husband in
the process—this way he became aware of her goals and her
transformation was not too big a surprise or shock.

The change in one person in the family or a group changes the entire relationship, and we need to appeal to the others' flexibility to evolve along with us. The fear that this might cause major discomfort or conflict usually keeps us stuck in our old behaviour.

However, fear is an emotion that is unique to humans. The purpose of fear is to protect us from danger, but often the danger is imagined. Our existential fears essentially go back to the fear of not being good enough, of being different, of not belonging, of not making a contribution, of not complying with societal norms.

Admiration for changes in appearance

Paradoxically, in some areas the threshold for enlisting the help of a coach is quite low. When we go to the gym, we don't hesitate to hire a fitness coach. If we want to lose weight we see a nutrition coach. When we are fitter and have lost weight we have a visible result. We look marvellous and we attract praise and admiration. We are proud of what we have achieved and we don't hesitate to mention the help we got from our fitness or nutrition coach.

The effects of mental coaching, however, are not really visible unless people say: "Your behaviour has changed." And those comments do not always make us happy. We are uneasy about internal change processes, because we no longer have control over the reactions they evoke. People around you often don't understand when you change inside. They might say things like: "Are you alright?" "Don't you think you should become normal again?" "Why don't you act like a regular person? You'd still be crazy enough."

Johan (44)

My wife has a new husband as a result of my coaching and the new awareness that I have gained. It is quite confusing for her, but she does appreciate that I am a better listener.

Jeanne (47)

When I talk with my sisters, I now give them a heads-up about my 'different' way of seeing things. I say: "I am going to tell you something and you will think it's crazy." And they just laugh at me. Is it my fault? It sure is. But I don't mind because I stand fully behind my idea. I chose it. What they think of it is their problem.

Dirk (36)

I always kept very quiet during meetings. I hired a coach to help me become more vocal. Finally, I was ready. I started with saying things like: "If I may summarise this ..." or, "If I understand correctly, this is about ...". Later I would add a comment or two. I was proud that I got this far. Thanks to coaching I now had the courage to speak. Unfortunately the first reaction I received was: "Wow, you must have had some kind of training, because you are suddenly so difficult to deal with." I can't say I enjoyed those comments.

Having others try to lure us back to our former behaviour can be a dreadful experience. As much as we might enjoy our newfound attitude, the resistance this provokes can have a sobering effect. Your change has a mirroring effect on others. When you change, you challenge others to address their flaws and habits. This is difficult for them, and they prefer to stick to the old way of doing things. So they give you a hard time. The risk is that you might take their attacks personally, when all their reaction shows is a reluctance to change themselves. They prefer to stay within their comfort zone.

What is wrong with comfort?

The only way a company can really change is if people dare to step out of their comfort zones. Continuing to do the same thing will bring the same result. Change happens at the border between comfort and discomfort. Therefore, if people want to change, you need to bring them to the brink of their discomfort. The status quo is like a down comfort blanket, nice and warm. Action begins only when you pull away that comfort blanket.

As a CEO it is best to encourage your employees to step out of their comfort zones, not least because innovation is key to keeping a competitive edge. It is essential for companies to evolve in every imaginable way and, if possible, create opportunities for themselves. The more a company evolves, the greater its need for growing awareness. The two go hand in hand.

For technically oriented companies, this can be particularly challenging. Employees with a technical profile by nature seek stability, order, clarity, standardisation. They tend to be more afraid of stepping out of their comfort zones; what lies beyond their known territory is by definition unstructured and not under their control. And all that is not under control can lead to mistakes and personal failure. Breaking through this mentality requires a hefty dose of coaching.

2. FEAR OF THE MIRROR OF SUCCESS AND PERFECTION

The coach as role model

Coachees often look at their coaches as role models. The coach is the specialist, the expert. The professional coach surely has his life on track. This impression is often confirmed if the coach is also a trainer. It creates the idea that he has it all beautifully sorted out: life, work, success.

Nothing can be further from the truth. Coaches too are deliberately working on their change processes, perhaps even more so than their coachees. That is why it is important that they also show vulnerability. However, this can create a sense of doubt in the coachee: "If my coach is still working on this, how much more will I have to go through?"

Julie, certified coach, in therapy herself

During a coaching training session that I gave, I admitted that I was in therapy to get a better handle on my work-life balance. You should have seen the expressions on their faces. Surprise all around. But why? You? In therapy? How can that be? I answered that I found it important to dig deeper into this subject, to find the underlying reasons for my behaviour and to find my way to lasting success. That's when I saw the fear in their eyes, as if they were thinking: My goodness, here is someone who has been coach for so long and she still does not have her life in order!

Does coaching ever come to an end?
Are you afraid of being condemned to being coached for the rest of your life? Ideally, we should get coaching several times during our lifetime. Roughly estimated: once each in our early 30s, 40s, 50s and 60s. Those are typically the phases in our lives when it is helpful to regain balance and reorient ourselves.

The stages of life

Daniel J Levinson's *The Seasons of a Man's Life*[5] outlines the following major themes for each stage of life.

Between 18 and 36, your main focus lies on achieving excellence, strength, speed, perseverance and results. You feel strong; you make important life decisions (relationship, house, children …). Around 28, many become restless and wonder what they need to achieve real success. Most men are still quite competitive and focused on short-term success. It is at that stage that they want to see proof of their success through promotions.

Between 36 and 47, you are a part of management or a group of experts in your organisation. You are becoming increasingly independent of others, and you are searching for a confirmation of your values. You still feel quite young, but the 20-somethings don't see you that way. Your focus is still primarily on 'doing and having', on proving that you were able to accomplish your dream. Personal achievement is an important goal.

Between 40 and 60, you notice an even greater difference. Like it or not, you are no longer a part of youth. At work, you are beginning to become an expert in your field. In your inner circle you are increasingly confronted with mortality. Your children are getting older and you are paying more attention to 'life itself'. Your focus changes from 'doing and having' to 'being'. You enjoy guiding or mentoring young people. Men are increasingly getting in touch with their 'female' qualities, such as listening and showing greater empathy. The focus is increasingly on how to build a better life for themselves and others.

Realising that we worked like a horse, often only to fulfil someone else's expectations is a mirror that is held up to all of us.

After 60, you begin to see things from a certain distance. You are literally moving closer to the edge of the circle. You are facing physical impairments. The fear that you can no longer add any value grows. However, grandchildren sometimes fill that void. Your sense of integrity is increasing. You can be who you are. After all, what do you have to lose?

Each one of these life stages brings about change, usually slowly, sometimes abruptly. Our thoughts and our self-image tend to get stuck in an earlier phase, while our bodies have moved on in their natural evolution. Everybody around us sees it coming long before we do. Our blind spots and all their attendant behaviours sometimes come back to haunt us.

3. FEAR OF YOUR LESS ATTRACTIVE OR DARK SIDES

What prevents us from really looking at ourselves? We are afraid to face our shadow sides. We consider as 'bad' all that is different from how we usually are or what we have always regarded as normal. Introspection may also reveal our many prejudices!

For example: *Yes, women have to work, but not too hard, or at least not all the time, or else it means they are too strong. Men have to be focused on success. Failing that, they are just pansies.*

We set up societal or social norms and judge those who do not fulfil these. But who says that these standards are acceptable?

Maria (50)

I have learned to say: "I am dominant." Others perceive dominance as something negative, but that is strictly their perception. Dominance works for me; I achieve quite a lot with it. By admitting that I am dominant, I can work on it. To evolve in a certain aspect of yourself, you have to first accept that it is there, that it is your trait, your way of doing things.

Coaching *should* bring out our extremes, and that is what we fear. But the more we try to cover them up, the more they want to manifest themselves in a negative form. We prefer to run away from our spectres, not realising that most of them are actually good qualities, albeit in an intense form.

Take, for example, someone who expresses his displeasure and frustration in an inadequate manner when things are not going his way. This is an expression of his trait to have things under control.

Once a person is aware of this, he can remind himself to reign in his behaviour and to give others some space.

Questions for reflection

Time for some reflection and exercise, using the questions below. Ideally, stop after each question and take your time to answer. This is not a test. Notice what effect, or concern, comes up as you answer honestly and calmly.

> Whom do you admire?
> Either in your personal and work environment, or those of historical importance (such as Gandhi or Joan of Arc) or famous figures (like Steve Jobs or Angelina Jolie). What do you admire in these people: which achievements, which talents, which values, which principles? And what does that say about you?

> What are your strongest aspects and talents, and to what extent have you applied them in your life?

> What would you like your colleagues to say about you in a farewell speech at the end of your career?

> What have been the happiest moments in your life so far? What made you so happy at those times? How many of these moments are you creating for yourself?

> If money or the risk of failure were not concerns, what would you do?

> If you had five more years to live, what would you do? Four years? Three years? Two years? One year? Six months?

> Who can guarantee that you will live longer than that? Why are you not putting into action the answers to the questions above? What is your fear? What is holding you back?

> If you had a magic wand and you could wish for three things, what would they be?

> What did you enjoy doing most when you were a child? To what extent have you stayed loyal to yourself or forced yourself to change? And how does that feel?

> Which aspect(s) of your hobby would you like to find in your daily work?

> Which three of the following verbs appeal to you the most?
accomplish – assist – alleviate – enforce – give away – build – lead – design – connect – communicate – create – defend – discover – animate – enthuse – motivate – coach – facilitate – heal – explain – inspire – integrate – shape – implement – think – relax – raise – teach – reform – simplify – protect – bring together – sustain – renew – preserve – understand – liberate – serve – write – refine – listen – help – set in motion – achieve – participate – expand – care for – offer – awaken – grow – support

4. FEAR THAT OTHERS MIGHT STAND IN THE WAY OF YOUR SUCCESS

We worry that by giving too much attention to our employees, we might lose sight of our core business; i.e. our ability to provide products and services. We are assuming that focusing on results and success precludes having a heart and an ear for people.

This polarity in thinking, however, is not doing us any good. It is not about people *or* results. It is about people *and* results. There have been times when people acted like machines; for instance, during the Industrial Revolution. Today, we know how important it is to take care of the individual. After all, it is these individuals who are responsible for delivering our products and services, and these same people can be a liability in offering our products and services.

Grass will not grow faster by pulling on the blades, but by paying attention to what it needs to grow. Rationally, we are all aware of this. So what are the limiting thoughts and feelings behind our need to keep focused on nothing but results?

Time for reflection

Read the following questions and stop after each to write down some key words that come up — without self-censorship.

> What would happen to your image if others spoiled the results?
> What would happen if you 'had to' admit that others did the work and you merely motivated them or coordinated the process?
> What do you think of people who make it a point of creating a caring and attentive work environment?
> What are they missing out on? What chances of success might they be passing up?

Notice what reactions are evoked in you. How judgemental are these reactions? And what does that say about what you find important and what instills fear in you?

5. FEAR OF GETTING TO KNOW YOURSELF

How good are we with self-disclosure; i.e. showing ourselves as we really are? How much energy do we spend every day on hiding behind a mask of perfection, success, beauty, indifference, knowing it all, harmony, modesty, crowd-pleasing ... ? We are desperately trying to portray ourselves as perfect but the moment you take down your mask, look at your strengths and weaknesses and let others see these sides of you, you hold a mirror up to them and that is true courage!

As long as you hide behind a mask, you are only fooling yourself. Others have to second-guess you to be able to work with you efficiently. Besides, you can't win this battle. The older you get, the more vulnerable you become.

The business world is taking note. Under the banner of 'authentic leadership', people are being encouraged to build on their strengths and to really get to know themselves. *Be who you are. No more, no less.* Employees are tired of a manager who is merely playing a role.

The more comfortable we become with this trend, the more we can show our human side, the less energy we need to put into pretending how strong we are, and the more energy we have to fully nurture our careers and the goals we want to achieve.

Koen (45)

Coaching helped me as a sales manager to become more aware of my strengths and weaknesses and to name them without self-criticism, without being harsh on myself. The results were unbelievable, because I allowed myself to acknowledge the way I am at any given moment and to identify areas in which I wanted to grow more, I created a different way of communicating with my sales team. For the first time, I heard examples of wonderful and challenging moments with clients. It also created a solid base for cooperation and interaction. I got the feeling that the phase of 'let's put up a façade, no matter what ... 'was finally over and that we could finally achieve better results. We now go to the root of the problems and stop covering up mistakes.

6. FEAR OF ABUSE OF TRUST

We fear that our private information may be used against us. We don't want them to know who we really are. We are doing our jobs and what we do in our private time is our business."

Our basic assumptions are that the less they know about us, the more they see of the exterior and the less they will talk behind our backs—until one day we expose ourselves accidentally. That is when they begin wondering, "What has he been hiding all this time?"

The younger generation appears to have fewer inhibitions about exposing themselves. On Facebook or other social media, for example, they say what they find important; they admit their mistakes, say what they have learned from their mistakes, and concede that they are not perfect. *So what?* seems to be the mantra.

Such a mentality leads to mutual trust (provided of course that everyone is on board). In 2012 (Turning Point year = Year of Acceleration), we were confronted with major differences in perception, particularly in the area of self-revelation. The older generation (baby boomers and Gen X) thinks the Y-generation (aged 20+) is too careless. They think that young people are too open with their opinions on Facebook and are concerned that it could damage their image. The younger generation finds that it no longer has to play that game. Authenticity counts. There are limits of course. All this openness should not be confounded with brutal criticism of others on other social media forums.

We still have much to learn from each other ...

Time for reflection

Let the following questions sink in before noting the key words of your answers.

> What would happen if people at work knew that you are going through a hard time at home because your rebellious teenagers are acting up?
> How would you feel if your boss confided in you that his partner told him off for working such long hours?
> What would be the effect if you found out that your colleague has a really unusual hobby?

Observe your internal reactions. How easy is it for you to deal with differences, or with revelations from others? What is the level, if any, of discomfort you are experiencing?

We are continually evolving towards a more diverse society, which requires greater inclusion and tolerance to function healthily. It is not surprising that we are having difficulties with this: historically we have always felt safest in homogeneous groups. The fear of not being safe is deep-seated. But how realistic is that fear today? We are captives of our own circle of fear. Fear breeds fear. Cruelty provokes more cruelty. Mistrust creates mistrust ...

It is a coach's job to mirror these phenomena. The choice is yours whether you want to examine them or not, and you decide whether it feels reasonable—and safe—to act on your insights.

7. FEAR OF DISCOVERING ALL YOUR TALENTS

When we are asked what we are good at, we often hesitate. This re-luctance may stem from the thought: *Will I come across as arrogant if I talk about my talents? Will they call me on it?* It is difficult to look at our weaknesses, but sometimes even harder to admit our strong points. This is what keeps us from utilising our full potential and from flourishing.

The following text by author and peace activist Marianne Williamson reminds us of the futility of keeping our talents in the shadows.

Your playing small does not serve the world ...

Our deepest fear is not that we are inadequate.
Our deepest fear is that we are powerful beyond measure.
It is our light, not our darkness that most frightens us.
We ask ourselves,
Who am I to be brilliant, gorgeous, talented, fabulous?
Actually, who are you not *to be?*
You are a child of God.
Your playing small does not serve the world.
There is nothing enlightened about shrinking so that other peo-ple won't feel insecure around you. We are all meant to shine, as children do.
We were born to make manifest the glory of God that is within us.
It's not just in some of us; it's in everyone. And as we let our own light shine, we unconsciously give other people permission to do the same.
As we are liberated from our own fear, our presence automati-cally liberates others.

A coach challenges you to face your true qualities, to name them without fear and to translate them into actions that lead to success. But here's the rub: do you dare to be highly successful? Do you dare to dazzle with your talents?

Imagine it was easy to really make a difference. Imagine getting into the flow and enjoying what you do and what you are capable of. What are some of the thoughts that come up? Now imagine that you have just realised that you kept your talents under cover all these years because they did not fit your study or career choice. What does this realisation do to you?

Working on your talents implies that you believe that you have talents that are unique. Ultimate fulfilment comes through fully tapping into all your talents and by letting them shine.

Such reflections require a lot of courage. You can't do this without help. The realisation that you have never really chosen for *yourself* is a hefty confrontation in itself.

8. FEAR OF ALLOWING YOURSELF TO BE HAPPY

True and profound happiness can be achieved only by using our talents and by listening to our hearts. However, many of us are afraid to show our happiness. We can find happiness in humour, in short moments of pleasure, but not beyond.

Complainers get more attention than those who are happy-go-lucky. Is it okay to be cheerful at work, even if things don't go smoothly all the time? Or will that cast us as simpletons or as someone who does not take his job seriously? Do you dare to simply be happy, in the here and now, without having to have a special occasion? You risk being labelled naïve, surely? After all, who are you to have no problems? It appears that displays of happiness can come across as a threat.

On the contrary, deliberate, pure happiness is contagious. It is true, though, that staying in touch with your own joyous core is not always easy.

9. FEAR OF BECOMING A DIFFERENT PERSON

Coaching supports you in achieving your full potential. Once you start, you will notice many changes in yourself and in your surroundings. You throw off ballast and begin to listen more to your own needs without hurting others. You are empowering yourself, you enjoy yourself and you shine.

When one element is changed it affects the entire system. The first negative reactions from others are usually nothing but a sign of their resistance to change.

Both my boss and my coach encourage me to become more assertive. But when I do so, I get an earful from my colleagues, as they must then do the tasks that I no longer will.
I also behave differently in meetings now. The first reaction was: "Don't change. You were already difficult enough to deal with." My change represents a challenge to them, because it forces them to evolve with me.
I am increasingly tapping into my strategic competencies and using my talents to think outside the box. But doesn't that mean I'm showing off, or showing others up? Am I then not raising the bar for my colleagues? How am I going to handle that?

Our behaviour holds up a mirror to others, which might at times be uncomfortable. However, if we believe that people are resilient and that everyone has the (secret) wish to use their potential to the fullest, then our decision to change serves as an inspiration for their growth.

10. FEAR OF LOSING SELF-CONFIDENCE

We live in constant fear of the consequences of our decisions. Some of our hidden thoughts may be: *what if I were to lose my partner as a result of becoming a different person? Who would I be then? What will be the effect on my image? What if I lose confidence in myself?*

Once you start to change, there may be moments when you lose your bearings. But who says that you have to be at peak confidence all the time? Wouldn't that make you somewhat arrogant? There is nothing wrong with having a dip in your confidence level every now and then. It leads you to think about what is essential and allows you to regroup. Paradoxically, periods of reduced confidence can lead to greater self-satisfaction, even if we only see this in hindsight.

We all try to avoid chaos, but coaching creates just that. Coaching provokes us so that we can sow fresh seeds. For some it may shake up self-confidence; others may regain trust in themselves.

11. FEAR OF CONFRONTING YOUR SELF-SABOTEUR

Like it or not, we all have self-sabotaging thoughts. The list of concerns at the beginning of this chapter proves just that. All those fears are self-sabotaging thoughts. We are often afraid, though, to look our self-saboteur in the eye.

Lila (38)

Lila had been saying that she wanted to follow a coaching course since 1992. She was convinced that it would help her better utilise her talents. She even completed a registration form a few years ago—but that was as far as she got. Last year was a terrible year for her. She made a bad investment, her financial situation turned sour and her relationship suffered. Finally she took the plunge and signed up for the course. Today she is choosing to focus on her talents. She is getting coaching to help her see how she can deal better with her pain and with the difficulties on her path.

How far do you have to be pushed before you begin to put yourself first? Which is the biggest culprit among your self-sabotaging thoughts? Lisa could have been much further along, but her self-saboteur said: "Watch out, you could fail." Ironically, that is what kept her from achieving success.

We desperately want success, but we tend to sabotage ourselves. It can feel better to stay stuck in the familiar than to take risks.

Equally paralysing, is the fear of having an impact on other people's lives; the fear that we might set something in motion that is bigger than ourselves. Or the fear that people may consider us strange, the fear of becoming isolated, of being seen as 'special'. If you use your talents to become successful, others may become jealous. How would we deal with that?

We often take out our lack of self-love on ourselves. We develop all kinds of aches and pains; we feel depressed; we have no drive; we fill up on unhealthy stimulants, knowing very well how harmful they are. If this behaviour gets out of hand, it can make us ill. And yet, we continue to sabotage ourselves. The mechanism behind this is simple: When we get ill and run into problems, we receive the attention we were craving. Attention can alleviate our pain or burden. Getting attention feels like a confirmation of our worth.

Do you recognise any of these self-sabotaging actions?
> Eating a piece of chocolate or cookies whenever you feel the slightest discomfort
> Lazing in the easy chair when you should be working in the garden
> Giving vague instructions, knowing this will lead to a poor outcome
> Refusing to ask for directions, knowing that you will arrive late anyway
> Not saying what you mean
> Driving too fast, despite knowing that it is dangerous (and/or could lead to a hefty fine)
> Passing another driver illegally
> Not filling up the petrol tank even though the needle is already on red
> Not checking the alarm clock and oversleeping
> Staying up too late and being in a bad mood the next day
> Not paying the bills and waiting for reminders
> Excessive drinking in the evenings despite having liver problems
> Gossiping, knowing that people will then also gossip about you

Do you tend towards procrastination, another mild form of self-sabotage?
> Not calling back and thereby causing frustration or conflict
> Not completing your tax returns
> Knowing you need to sew on a button, but then losing it before you get around to it
> Sending birthday cards late

> Knowing you should back-up your data, but then losing it before you decide to do it

Procrastination is a huge waste of time and energy. When we procrastinate we spend two to ten times more time and effort thinking about what we need to do. It spoils our mood, our free time, our concentration.

Can you relate to any of these self-sabotaging thoughts?
> I will embarrass myself again
> I am sure something will come up to prevent this. Why go through the trouble?
> It's not going to last anyway
> I will never be able to do that
> I can't afford this
> You can't trust anybody
> I have no patience for that
> I am too old for this
> I have always been bad at languages
> Arriving late, that's my modus operandi

Whenever you hear yourself say, "I am ... ", be alert! Is what you intend to say next going to undermine yourself?
> That's how I am
> I am inept
> I am lazy by nature
> I am who I am and I won't change
> I am not attractive
> I am not good at friendships
> I am sloppy
> I am good for nothing

And also watch out for sentences that begin with "why".

> Why did I let this happen again?
> Why should I try again?
> Why do I keep telling myself that I can do this?
> Why should I be allowed to participate?

All this worrying, and constantly asking yourself questions to which there are no answers, consumes a lot of energy. When we can't find the answer, we need to let go of the question and take it up again some other time.

Everyone has their own variations of the above. Self-sabotaging thoughts and actions are driven by your subconscious. It may feel as if you have no control over them. A coach can help you work through those thoughts and become more aware of them. This will help you move a big step forward: as soon as you become aware of things, you can begin to influence them.

II. GUILT: BARRIER OR MOTIVATOR?

What gives you the energy to stick it out in your job? To take on yet another assignment? To stay on those extra hours to finish a task? Is it because failing to do so would make you feel guilty?

At first glance, it may seem as if guilt pushes us forward. Your guilt motivates you to work overtime and go the extra mile to make sure you are worth your money.

However, if you take a closer look at your feelings of guilt, you quickly notice that they prevent you from performing at your best. Guilt is always linked to self-judgement. The thoughts behind guilt are: *I am too lazy; I am not analytical enough; I am not available enough; I am not strong enough; I don't perform well enough* ... In other words, *I am not worthy.*

Guilty feelings rob you of your energy. They keep you from enjoying each moment. Somewhere in the back of your mind, you keep asking yourself, *what am I entitled to? What am I capable of?* and *what do I want?*

Dealing with guilt is one of the top coaching themes, because the emotions linked to guilt are more inhibiting than motivating. Emotions evoke physical reactions and can lead to tunnel vision. Business managers need to have a clear picture, keen insight and make solid decisions. Feelings of guilt are more of a barrier than a benefit. Emotions that remain unaddressed cloud the mind and get in the way of setting boundaries. The only way to regain clarity of thinking is by taking away the force of the emotion—by listening to it kindly.

Some executives are afraid to accept a promotion because they fear that it will lead to even longer hours and more stress. The fact that they don't know how to set boundaries restricts them in their opportunities.

What comes up for you when looking at the following? What if you went for a promotion without feeling guilty?

> What if you accepted a promotion but insisted on establishing your limits and refused to work longer hours?
> What if you managed to utilise your expertise and strengths fully within these limits?
> What if you needed those limits for optimal performance?
> What if you were then truly motivated? Could you believe in that?

III. THE SOURCE OF OUR FEARS: A NEED TO BE APPRECIATED

Our behaviour and performances are often not appreciated unless they have been based on huge effort, unless they cost us blood, sweat and tears. Things that do not require much effort are considered a matter of course and do not receive much attention. Above all we are looking to fill the 'gap' to be successful, to feel well, happy, and content.

At the bottom of our fears there lies a universal need to
> be appreciated for who we are
> be recognised for our strengths and talents
> belong
> contribute in a meaningful way
> be happy and content

We strive hard to fulfil these needs and yet we keep running into roadblocks. Looking back at our achievements might not be helpful in filling these needs. What is more, looking at what others have achieved appears to be the mirror for our own (lack of) progress. So, might it be better to look at what others have not yet accomplished?

Sincere appreciation begins with paying attention

The simplicity of validation

Validation, a short film by Kurt Kuenne (http://www.youtube. com/watch?v=Cbk980jV7Ao 16:24 min) tells the story of Hugh, a man who validates parking tickets—and the customers he serves. He gives a sincere compliment to each surprised customer, who leaves with a smile and a good feeling. Soon clients are queuing up at the parking garage. When Hugh needs to renew his driver's license, he runs into Victoria, the only person whom he cannot manage to make smile ...

Validation is a film about a special form of attention, namely recognising people for who they are. Recognition is essential for us to function. The human touch that goes hand in hand with sincere recognition is like fuel for a motor. It sets everything in motion but it is equally important to be open to being appreciated, to take the time to receive appreciation and be thankful for it. As the reactions of the people in *Validation* shows, this is not easy. Many of these individuals become emotional. Is this because of their inability to recognise appreciation or to accept it? We believe both are the case. We are all craving recognition. Validating attention helps people appreciate themselves more. To open up to others then becomes much easier.

This does not mean that as a manager you have to constantly shower your employees with compliments to win them over but it does mean that you need to make a point of appreciating their strengths as much as highlighting their areas for improvement. Validating people means that you appreciate them for who they are. There is no need for glorification, but put-downs are certainly not acceptable.

Up-coaching of managers

Don't managers need to be appreciated too? Where do they get recognition from? Don't they have the right to be appreciated by their employees? The reality is that bosses are rarely told what is good about them. Employees might admit among each other that their boss is not so bad, but telling him to his face is often a big step.

Ilse, project manager

I had my annual evaluation with my boss—not something I was looking forward to. The conversation went really well, in contrast to previous discussions we've had. In the past I had the feeling that we were on different wavelengths. We both ended up being irritated with each other, discussed (read: argued) heartily, only to discover that we usually wanted to achieve the same thing. And even then we continued to argue. This time was different though, even though we didn't agree on everything. At the end of the chat, I asked whether he had any further comments. He didn't. I said: "Wim, thank you for this discussion. I found it really pleasant."

My boss was really surprised. He didn't know how to react. He had a look of suspicion on his face, as if he was thinking, is this another of her cynical jokes? I confirmed with sincerity that I had found the talk constructive and appreciated his comments. He thanked me and gave me a warm smile. That felt good. I promised to myself that, in the future, I would pay more attention to his strong points and show my appreciation. It has improved our working relationship a great deal.

Whether we are managers or employees, we all have a need for recognition. We all make efforts and want to be appreciated for it. We must not deny that need. The fact that a little film like *Validation* has touched so many is proof enough.

IV. CHANGE REQUIRES COURAGE AND FOCUS

Do you have the courage to break your old habits?
Do you have the courage to learn to listen to the voices around
you instead of clinging to your own truths?
Do you have the courage to believe that 'the truth' does not
exist and that everything is perception?

Coachees come to coaches with their own convictions. As long as they continue to see the world according to their fixed mental models, they will continue to approach the world in the same old way, which often earns them nothing but resistance and obstruction.

A coach will challenge you with questions such as: "How sure are you of this?" or "What makes you think so?"

One of the future top managers in a consulting firm is
undergoing a 360° feedback process. Through his colleague's
feedback he learns that he does not listen; that he is not taking
others into consideration; that he comes across as a bulldozer.
He is stunned. As someone who is quite sure of himself, he
is convinced the others are wrong. What effect does such
behaviour have on the other employees? Do you have the
courage to challenge your convictions through the input from
others? Are our convictions really the only certainties we
can fall back on? Is everything as certain as we have always
believed?

Change can be achieved only through intensively and consistently creating new mental patterns. People who have been standing at an assembly line for years, doing the same thing day in and day out, have built strong conclusions about how the world works, excluding all possibilities that it could be any different. They function on auto-pilot and no longer reflect on what they are doing. Inspiring these individuals to begin thinking on their own feet again is hard work. For many executives, this is a special challenge: "How can I encourage people who have settled into execution mode—who I have rewarded for that behaviour for years—to evolve towards a mindset of participation, reflection and creativity?" This kind of transformation requires a solid change process that cannot be accomplished merely through a system of rewards and punishments.

We know that changing habits requires a lot of time and attention. Once you commit to change you bump up against your old behavioural patterns. Only through continuous focus on your new way of thinking—for about 50 consecutive days—and with the support of your colleagues and others, can you create new neural connections in your brain, replacing the old.

Training and coaching can teach you to deal with these changes and accompany you while taking into consideration the various personality types. It is only natural that you will come up against self-judgement and limiting beliefs. Breaking through mental barriers to deal with change is the first step for each executive. A coach will be happy to assist with these issues.

Walter Verhelst
– European Controlling Department, Chartis Europe SA

I arrived at a point in my career where I no longer enjoyed being an executive, but instead felt the urge to inspire people. I had been working with numbers all my life—a bit like a historian who is meticulously recording all events and writing up an accurate report. These figures were my crystal ball or the tea leaves that helped me predict future trends; they were the instruments to guide the company in a certain direction.

But after a while the novelty was gone, and the exercise became an annual and quarterly routine. I started to wonder whether the purpose of all these stories I was telling my employees was merely to convince them of my ways and weaken their arguments. That's when I no longer wanted to continue and I experienced emotions for the first time in my work. I thought it was a sign of getting older.

And then I saw a coach. I learned to understand myself better and to look at others from a different angle. Their words became subordinate to their actions. I learned to interpret reactions in a way that helped me leverage them to accomplish things, whereas before these same reactions had been blocking me.

Intense conversations about practical matters brought up all kinds of norms and values that were important for me. I had encountered these concepts before in literature, philosophy, through joy and happiness gurus, but in the conversations with the coach they became tangible, simple and clear.

Coaching has taught me to understand my reactions, and as a result I can understand my colleagues and their way of seeing things. I was finally able to give them the feeling that they had accomplished something while I had merely guided them.

The prerequisites to becoming successful are: to know yourself and know what you are capable of, but also to have unconditional respect for your fellow man, allowing him to unleash his talents in a common project and to accomplish it all without pressure, and only through motivation. This revelation has made me a richer, smarter, but above all, happier person.

In the past, I led a department. Today I manage a project that stretches across Europe. I have no authority. All I have is my knowledge and my skills. Above all I have a deeper understanding of myself and of the people I work with, even those who I never see.

4

Out of the
mental rut

PART 4

OUT OF THE MENTAL RUT

Georges Anthoon is a former HR Director at AXA Belgium and author of the bestseller *Talent in Action*. He is also a coach. In this chapter, he talks candidly about his own experiences with coaching. He will focus on the competencies of a good coach and, based on these competencies, explain the impact coaching has had on his management style and on him as a person, partner and father. Coaching—and managing with a coaching attitude—will always set something in motion and trigger a positive dynamic, both in business and in private.

For a long time, managing employees meant passing on the lessons and management tools I had learned and telling my employees, based on my experiences, how to function. My role was to be the 'answering machine' for all questions and the 'problem-solving machine' for all issues that came up.

Most managers have a similar approach. They usually find themselves in a *telling mode*: "Do this, don't do that", or "This won't work, but this will." Sometimes this approach is useful and employees appreciate it. However, there is a lot more to *coaching* employees than that. Coaching is first and foremost a personal attitude. It comes down to the firm belief that thoughts and actions can be changed and that we can help people develop their potential by asking them questions; i.e. by being in an *asking mode* rather than by giving them answers. I have learned that the best way to develop this attitude is by going through a coaching process yourself.

By experiencing what it means to be coached, you develop the ability to stay in motion; to set others in motion; to have the courage to ask questions out of a state of not knowing; and to make mistakes and learn from them. My personal coaching journey and International Coaching Federation (ICF) certification process [see below] developed both my hunger for feedback (i.e. what I can learn from the past) and feed-forward (i.e. what I can learn from this for the future).

Falling and getting back up

To become and to be a coach—and thus also to become and be a manager-coach—is a process of falling and getting up again. It means questioning yourself constantly to allow yourself to continue to grow as a person and a manager. It is a permanent process of change.

To step into this process as a manager is a serious challenge, but it adds tremendous value, both for yourself and for your enterprise.

I too belonged to the group of executives who was convinced that they did not need a coach—until I did my coaching certification training at The Coaching Square, where Leen Lambrechts and Marleen Boen, the co-authors of this book, resolutely held up the mirror to me. Suddenly, I realised how much each of us needs a trusted external person to help us get rid of our old ways of thinking.

The metaphor we often use in coaching is that of the farmer who rides his tractor to the field each day along the same path. By consistently taking this path, the grooves of his tracks become deeper and deeper, until finally it becomes nearly impossible to change tracks. We all have these mental ruts or rather, established beliefs.

There is nothing wrong with beliefs in themselves: beliefs are often a solid base for approaching the world. It's just that some of our solutions and approaches have exceeded their expiration dates. The world around us changes all the time and we therefore need be ready to adjust in an instant.

"Changed"

I began my coaching studies in 2008, ostensibly with the goal of receiving my certificate as a professional certified coach from the International Coaching Federation (ICF). My stated objectives were to learn more techniques to become a better coach. During that period, the notion was born that I could potentially work as an internal coach at AXA for all its top executives across Europe. The HR director at the time was in favour of that idea. After all, I could not be the HR director for Belgium forever, as internal management tried to rotate executive jobs on a regular basis. In my case, that would have meant a job abroad, which at the time I could not accept for personal reasons. I was prepared, however, to travel abroad on a regular basis to perform assessments and coaching sessions for executives.

In 2010, it became clear that the group HR department in Paris no longer supported that plan. We therefore agreed mutually and amicably that we would go our separate ways.

What struck me, though, was that, from the time I started my coaching training until my departure from AXA, my employees noticed "certain changes in me ... " At first, I was not quite sure what they meant.

My employees had tended to appreciate my decisiveness and energy, strategic vision, solution-oriented approach, profound knowledge about HR matters, motivational qualities and strong communication skills.

But increasingly, they began to mention aspects that had not been there before, such as "really listening"; daring to show feelings; asking others for input instead of always trying to find the solution myself; showing a quieter and more reflective attitude towards others; and alternating my telling mode with an asking mode. These are all themes that had come up during my coaching training.

There is no better mirror of your own reality (read: blind spots), as an individual or an executive, than coaching because once you are at an executive level, no one dares to really confront you anymore about your shortcomings.

Out of the comfort zone
Thanks to all the executive coaching I have been privileged to perform in the past years, I can draw on a wealth of stories that have come out of my sessions with top managers.

A large number of them have become emotional leaders, much to their own satisfaction and that of their companies. People whose companies offered coaching to them as one last chance to become more people-oriented leaders seemed completely changed after only 6 to 9 months. The dismissal papers that were waiting in the drawer were happily torn up. The nicest compliment came from Jean Marie (the HR director of a large telecommunications firm): "We don't know what kind of pills you gave to your coachee, but we are extremely happy with his evolution."

Just to make things clear: Coaches don't give pills. We ask questions that let the coachee see things from a different perspective; *we bring people out of their comfort zones so that they can bring about change in themselves.* In short: the coach facilitates and the coachee works towards his new goals.

Others come away with a completely different set of leadership tools by connecting more emotionally with their teams. These executives ended up with a dream team in which everyone willingly went through the fire for one another and kept each other focused by being brutally honest and by holding up mirrors to each other.

A particularly special story regards Luc, CEO of an HR service company, who decided that every executive should receive coaching training. The company culture changed completely, because executives ended up interacting with each other in completely different ways, and all of them began to apply a coaching approach in their management style. Luc argues that people who work in an environment where everyone likes to go to work and is given space to grow and use his talents, are better performers.

Luc is the archetype of a modern authentic leader who functions as a director of an orchestra and who does not play an instrument himself. And there is no need for the latter: his employees are empowered and they know that he stands squarely behind them should they need support. Luc is also a lot more balanced as a person than in the past, and his organisation can feel it. None of this prevents him and his team from achieving respectable results in a socially responsible manner.

Experience is not enough
I met Marleen Boen and Leen Lambrechts for the first time in 2005, while searching for a talent and coaching programme for high potential and senior managers at AXA Belgium.

During my discussion with them, I hinted at the possibility of working as a coach, hoping that they would be interested in someone with the experience of a seasoned manager, someone with a lot of miles behind him. To be honest, I expected my proposal to be met with enthusiasm, but instead I encountered reservation and conditions.

Their first suggestion was that I get my certification as a coach. And there it was: rejection—or at least, that's what it felt like— of my ambition to get involved in talent development, despite more than 30 years of experience as a senior manager and executive. Talk about confrontation!

A list of arguments followed: "A coach can be a coach only if he has experienced what it means to be coached. Coaching is more than telling people what to do based on your experience. Asking the right questions and actively listening, two attitudes indispensable to becoming an effective coach, is not something you learn at leadership courses." And those were just a few of the reservations they struck me with.

In mid-2010, I signed up for the training programme—more because large companies tend to require certification as proof of quality than out of the belief that I needed to develop my coaching competencies. Today, I understand: only those who have experienced coaching themselves can know as a coach what kind of impact it can have on individuals.

Some may argue that certification is unnecessary; that is up for debate. What I do know, however, is what the certification programme has done for me; it has made me a much better coach, mentor, trainer, person, father, husband and manager.

All former participants will attest to how much of an impact such a programme has had on their functioning as a coach, manager and person, and how it allows you to discover your own model of the world (i.e. your own set of beliefs, visions, ideas, values, and drives).

Having acquired that insight you can begin working with the coachee's model of the world, without the slightest (pre)judgement. This basic attitude of "being comfortable in not knowing and not judging" allows coachees to come up with their own solutions, based on their own background and value patterns rather than on the coach's ready-made vision. *Mastering the right coaching technique is a difficult process, but it offers you the chance to rediscover yourself.*

To illustrate this point further, I will describe to you the ICF's '11+1 core competencies'. I will provide you with an overview of the subjects that covered during a certification programme and elaborate on what coaching training has brought me and the impact it has had on my life.

COMPETENCIES 1 AND 2
ESTABLISHING A COACHING FRAMEWORK AND A COACHING CONTRACT

A coach has to adhere to the ethical and professional standards of the ICF, which include aspects like confidentiality and respect. A coachee's manager or HR director is often curious to find out what has been discussed during the coaching conversations, but of course they will not get any insight into these discussions from the coach.

I have learned as a coach the importance of establishing a clear framework at the outset of the coaching process and to set up clear agreements between coach and coachee. Among the things we determine is whether the interactions should have more of a consulting, mentoring or 'real' coaching character. In addition, I clearly explain the differences between coaching and therapy.

A good coaching framework leads to an appropriate coaching plan. People like to know where they are, where they are going in their coaching process, and what they should and should not expect. A good itinerary is the first step towards a successful coaching journey.

COMPETENCY 3
BUILDING AN OPEN AND TRUSTING ENVIRONMENT FOR LEARNING

This competency is about establishing an environment for a *co-creative partnership*. It is all about the importance of showing respect for the perceptions of the client, his learning style and his individual way of being. It seems logical, but is easier said than done. We all have our own models of the world, our own frame of reference, our own experiences and contexts, and it is therefore rather tempting to direct the coachee from our stance.

Naturally, the coachee also has his own model of the world and context. What appeared to be a great solution in the past, and in coach's context, may be inappropriate in the coachee or employee's situation. A spoiler is a great idea for a Formula 1 race car, because it helps the car maintain its grip on the track at high speed, but it is completely useless on the back of a turtle. Unfortunately, this was exactly the coaching style I subconsciously, and with best intentions, adhered to as a manager.

In other words, it is important for a coach to act from a point of neutrality; i.e. without (pre)judgement, something that appears easier in theory than it is in reality. We practised this skill over and over with each other during our coaching training. We repeatedly came up against thoughts that prompted questions from our own context and vision. Shutting out these thoughts and simply building on what the coachee says requires tremendous effort and practice. Actively listening is vital too (see Competency 5). Your questions should be built solely on what has been said and not based on your inner voice. This is possibly the most difficult learning aspect throughout the entire coaching training. Mastering this skill took the greatest effort of all.

It is also essential to the way you give suggestions and ideas to your coachee. In the past, I had the audacity to suggest one idea, based on my own experience as the only valid one. Today I take a completely different approach. There is nothing wrong with giving your coachee suggestions or sharing your experiences; it depends on *how* you do it, though. I have learned to put all the tips and tricks on the table (literally) and to give coachees the chance to examine these and see what would work for them. This allows coachees to choose their own solutions, which helps them in the long run to increase their independence. There is another advantage to having the coachee making his own decisions: he will be more inclined to follow through on his own solutions. The chance of follow-through is considerably smaller when answers are ready-made and from external sources.

Learning from golf

My British golf teacher, Robert, is a master at letting his players make their own analysis of their game (and above all, their faults) and in doing so, finding their own solutions. Most golf trainers have the tendency to overwhelm their trainees with comments about what went wrong after each bad hit. Robert has a completely different approach. After every good ball or bad ball I would get the question: "Georges, what do you think really happened here? What was right? What was wrong? What will you concentrate on next time? What will you start practicing more?"

In the beginning I found these questions annoying. I answered, "I don't know, you are the trainer!" But gradually I saw the parallels between his approach and that of the company coach: letting the coachee learn and reflect on his game or situation; creating a learning environment that allows for a co-creative partnership. This allows you to correct yourself during that first competition, when, of course, he is not on hand, when you are technically and mentally dependent on yourself.

Creating a confidential learning environment also implies that the coach asks the coachee's permission to coach in sensitive areas, or before confronting the coachee with one of his limiting beliefs. This was one of the biggest eye openers during my training. I completely underestimated the power of this approach. Strangely enough, coachees never, or hardly, ever refused such a request. Questions such as "Are you ready to talk about this sensitive issue now?" often bring coachees into the right frame of mind to tackle the subject. I am surprised every time at how suddenly all resistance or defensive behaviour falls by the wayside. The client is always in charge and that creates a sense of trust.

Another important skill for a coach is the ability to adjust one's pace to that of the coachee. I used to find this difficult too. My ex-employees used to describe me as someone who liked to spring into action. That is, in fact, my life and work rhythm. In the past, I found it hard to stand still and often thought that others were too slow, which of course implied an unjust value judgement. The secret is to treat people the way they want to be treated, rather than treating them according to your own pace and life vision. It took a lot of work to acquire this skill—and it remains an issue for me.

COMPETENCY 4

BEING FULLY PRESENT AND CREATING A SPONTANEOUS, OPEN, FLEXIBLE AND TRUSTING RELATIONSHIP WITH THE COACHEE

Being fully present is essentially about concentrating 100% during coaching. Coachees can tell you an important detail at any given moment. Every conversation requires of the coach his utmost attention to be able to ask the right questions and maintain a proper attitude. You cannot allow yourself as a coach to have your thoughts somewhere else.

Another important aspect of this competency is that you need to be open to *not knowing* and to taking the risk of asking what might at first sight seem an awkward question—all motivated by a great sense of curiosity. I remember vividly how strange this felt to me the first few times. *How competent can I be as a coach if I don't grasp quickly what the coachee's problem is? Or if I don't have any answers to his questions?* Today I know better: a coach is merely the facilitator of bringing things in motion within the coachee, based on the coachee's increased awareness. Once you have mastered that skill, you can manage a host of different situations.

This mindset has come in handy particularly in my work as an external manager of companies, as a senior trainer with Management Centre Europe and as HR and change consultant. Questions such as, "Tell me what is so difficult for you in this situation" or, "What thoughts or feelings are coming up for you when you say this?" or, "How did you arrive at this insight or belief?" always provide a wealth of information which you would otherwise have missed. In the past, it was important for me to grasp things quickly. Today I insist on questioning until the real reasons or limiting beliefs/thoughts emerge.

Creating a trusting environment also includes the dimensions below. As I had already used these skills quite well and intuitively, they were an area of minor development for me.

> *Using humour and lightness to create energy.* I quickly discovered that humour can help break the ice in heavy negotiations with the unions, especially after discussions have become heated.
> *Changing perspectives and confidently experimenting with different methodologies.* Employees told me that I had a talent for always looking for new solutions, off the beaten track, or for developing new things. A coach has a vast repertoire of exploration methods at his disposal.
> *Projecting a sense of self-esteem in situations where the client shows strong emotions and giving your own emotions their proper place without letting go of or distorting the process.* I have always had a healthy dose of self-confidence, and I am quite good at keeping a cool head. An area for improvement for me is to avoid putting the coachee's feelings into perspective too quickly.

COMPETENCY 5
ACTIVELY LISTENING AND BEING ABLE TO FOCUS ON WHAT THE COACHEE SAYS (OR DOES NOT SAY)

It is well known that *actively listening* is a challenge for people who tend to have a telling attitude. The pitfall for extroverted individuals is talking too much and listening too little. Introverts do the exact opposite. Not knowing what an extrovert thinks means that you did not listen well enough (because he will be quick to tell you his opinion); not knowing what an introvert thinks means that you did not ask enough questions (because they tend to wait until someone asks their opinion).

This was in fact one of my greatest personal challenges, but I am happy that I have found my way. This coaching skill helps me make a difference in my other types of work.

An imperative under this competency is that the coach strictly follows the coachee's agenda rather than his own. In your early days as a coach you might well fall into the trap of directing the coachee towards a solution that you would have chosen for yourself were you in his position. In principle, it is not wrong to have ideas about a certain topic or to bring them up at a suitable moment in the conversation. It all depends on the coachee's objectives and how he sees himself achieving these objectives within his specific context. Let him figure out ways and means by himself and, if needed, present him at the right moment with new approaches as a non-binding suggestion.

It is the coach's job to explore, consider and validate concerns, objectives, values and beliefs from the coachee's perspective. A good coach accepts what the coachee expresses in terms of feelings, perceptions, needs, values, and ideas.

And herein lies the crux of the matter. *I would never have thought instinctively that beliefs play such a huge role in the behaviour of people.* People are often not aware of their beliefs. As coachees gain greater clarity through your questions of their subconscious beliefs and logic, they become more aware of why they do or don't do certain things. Had I not followed a coaching training programme, I would have continued to coach people purely from a telling mode. I would never have learned to first detect the belief, then question it further and finally let the coachee explicitly rephrase it to give him a chance to work with it. This important lesson has prepared me well for my role as a change consultant. I have a much clearer understanding of how to approach resistance to change.

Only about 16% of people can be convinced of the need, rationale and background for change simply by explaining that need to them and by giving them detailed information. (See the study by Luc Dekeyser[7] and Everett Rogers). In other words, just giving them knowledge and insight about an impending change is sufficient for that group. By contrast, 68% of the average business population needs more than clarification and information. For these individuals to buy into the need for change, they need to be listened to, they need to be involved in the change process, and they must be supported during the implementation of these changes.

How many companies do you know that work that way? Are you still surprised to encounter resistance to change on the work floor? Don't we sometimes expect an awful lot of our employees?

> *"Management teams think about strategy for six months. They take six weeks to put strategy on paper. In six days they try to convince their direct reports. In six hours they tell it to the troops. The troops have six minutes to understand ... and six seconds to ask questions."*
> **– Business magazine**

Understanding this has been a real breakthrough in how I deal with resistance to change in my role as a change manager and change consultant. People on the work floor have all kinds of reactions, thoughts and limiting beliefs about how changes will affect their own situation. As a result, each one of them has a personal reaction towards the changes. A one-size-fits-all communication or approach does not make sense in this context. The only way to effectively manage resistance to the impending change is to listen to the individuals' concerns, involving them and examining the consequences, advantages and disadvantages of the change with them.

Two crucial sub-skills of active listening are *paraphrasing* and *restating*. The power of restating what has been said can never be underestimated. Since my coaching training, I consistently use this restating technique as a manager and as a coach. Try it out, and you will discover how much people appreciate it when they feel really listened to.

COMPETENCY 6
ASKING POWERFUL QUESTIONS THAT LEAD TO AWARENESS OF, AND RESPONSIBILITY FOR, THE DESIRED OUTCOME

Acquiring this competency was an enormous learning experience for me. This is one of the areas where the most learning and expansion happens. The ICF's definitions of powerful questions are:
> Questions that reflect active listening and an understanding of the coachee's perspective
> Questions that evoke discovery, insight, commitment or action (for example, by making limiting beliefs visible)
> Open questions that encourage greater clarity and new possibilities
> Questions that move the coachee forward towards his self-defined goal

These questions epitomise the purpose of coaching: setting people in motion through a heightened self-awareness which they acquire by means of questions that open their eyes and change their way of thinking. Every coach should espouse the following motto: "The key to wisdom is ... knowing all the questions" (*John A. Simone, Sr., American author and literary, theatre and film critic*)

Does this mean that the coach may no longer bring ideas or visions into the coaching conversation? Of course not. But it is important to choose the proper way and the right timing, and should never be done until the coachee has gained solid self-insight. A suggestion should never be stated as a "take it or leave it", but is meant to be examined for viability in the coachee's context.

COMPETENCY 7
ENSURING DIRECT AND CLEAR COMMUNICATION

The coach must be able to spell out the objectives of his coaching exercises and techniques and communicate them to the coachee clearly when establishing the session's agenda. In doing so, it is important that the coach uses appropriate and respectful language. It goes without saying that all language should be free of sexist, racist or potentially confusing technical comments.

Another key way to strengthening communication lies in *the power of naming things*. I discovered the tremendous value in openly and directly expressing certain things during a conversation, such as your own feelings, thoughts and impressions, or the things you notice about the coachee's body language or his (emotional) reactions ... Honest, direct and, sometimes, even explicit feedback aimed at respectfully stimulating the coachee can prompt enormous progress and heightened insight. In fact, people sometimes don't get going unless they are consistently shaken up. Sometimes this can lead to tension or strong emotions in the moment, but it won't fail to have a positive effect later on. Some people have a soft image of coaching, but nothing could be further from the truth! A coach is trained to provide support as best as he can and to confront firmly and respectfully if or when he has to.

Another core aspect of clear communication is the ability to make the coachee see things from a different perspective. We call this *re-framing*. I use this technique a lot in my personal life when confronted with a setback or an unexpected situation; I consistently reframe it according to my positive attitude to life. I ask questions, such as, *what can I learn from this situation? How can I best deal with this? What is positive in this situation? How can I see things from a different perspective?* The coachee should find his own way of reframing, based on your questions. Imposed reframing does not work.

COMPETENCY 8

PROMOTING AWARENESS IN THE COACHEE REGARDING HIS CHOSEN OBJECTIVE

My coaching training has helped me make a giant leap forward in creating greater awareness in coachees. Through spontaneous and intuitive practice on myself, this competency has evolved into a systematic coaching process consisting of various steps: identifying limiting beliefs, fears or barriers; laying the link to the coachee's underlying value patterns; exposing these elements by asking the coachee targeted questions; inviting the coachee to step out of this mental rut and evolve towards (other and new) empowering beliefs. All these steps are geared towards empowering the coachee to achieve his coaching objectives.

The following example illustrates how this works. Imagine a coachee who says he wants to stop smoking, but worries that he won't manage to do so. The coach's first intervention is to reformulate the objective together with the coachee. We all know that negative goals don't work. It is better to let the coachee state a positive objective, such as: "I want a healthier lifestyle" (which might include quitting smoking). After that, coach and coachee explore effective and non-effective (smoking) behaviour together. This allows the coachee to see the 'before' and 'after' of his way of thinking and feeling. Underlying thoughts and beliefs are then explored and listed; for example: "It will be difficult for me" or, "It will be hard for me to stop smoking as long as my partner continues".

Next we try to uncover the real underlying needs (perhaps: "I have to have something in my hands when I am stressed"). Finally, coach and coachee examine how the need and the objective can be combined: how can the coachee fulfil his need to have something in his hands in moments of stress and still quit smoking? The coachee then needs to find alternatives. Once he has discovered them, he can turn the limiting belief or fear ("I won't manage it") into an empowering belief ("Now that I have this alternative to smoking in stressful situations, I am able to quit.")

COMPETENCY 9
TOGETHER WITH THE COACHEE, IDENTIFYING ACTIONS, PROMOTING ACTIVE EXPERIMENTATION AND SELF-DISCOVERY AND OFFERING SUGGESTIONS THAT ARE IN LINE WITH THE COACHEE'S OBJECTIVES

As mentioned earlier, nurturing the coachee's independence is key—and extends also to designing his own actions. Self-formulated objectives and approaches lead to better results than imposed goals. It is a well-known fact in applied psychology that employee productivity decreases when change is imposed unilaterally. Productivity increases again the moment the workers become involved in the new work processes. The highest levels of productivity are achieved when workers have a say in the area they have an impact on.

Perhaps you have experienced this in your own life: it is much easier to follow through when it is *you* who makes the decision than if someone else tells you to do so. Managers should keep this in mind at all times, because herein lies the central thought behind empowerment: providing employees with the autonomy to determine their own approach, all within the company's boundaries and objectives.

In my capacity as HR and team manager, I have always believed in the importance of both trust and employee autonomy. I have evolved, however, in how and when I put my vision, solutions and approaches on the table. In the past, I would be rather quick to do so. Today, I leave my own answering and solution machines on stand-by, until I feel that my coachees are stuck and that they may benefit from my getting them back on track.

COMPETENCIES 10 AND 11
BUILDING AN ACTION PLAN WITH THE COACHEE AND MONITORING HIS PROGRESS AND PROCESS

Vision without action is but a daydream and leads to nothing. This has long been my motto as an HR manager and manager of change projects. It was therefore one of my more minor development areas during my coaching journey. However, through my coaching practice I discovered that I too frequently assumed that others are as action-oriented and decisive as I am.

I noticed that some coachees were very enthusiastic when they left their coaching sessions. They were flying high with their great ideas, but when you took a meet again a month later, they had hardly taken any action. This is when I decided that I needed to be more strict with my coachees. When a company pays for a coaching programme, the least that can be expected of a coachee is that he will take full advantage of it. This is why Competency No. 11 requires coaches to confront their coachees about any issues of self-discipline and achievement of defined results within a timeframe.

COMPETENCY 11 PLUS 1
DEMONSTRATING SELF-AWARENESS AND ATTENTIVENESS AS A COACH TO THE IMPACT OF YOUR OWN INTERVENTIONS AND AREAS OF DEVELOPMENT

Coaching has had a strong impact on my professional life, as well as on how I function every day and upon my interactions with others. To learn how to deal with feedback about your way of working in a constructive manner and to openly reflect on your behaviour are two fundamental issues and components of this continuous learning process. They have become a way of being for me, with an eye on my own continuous development as coach, consultant, manager, and as a person.

The above competencies were huge assets to me in obtaining results as a manager, trainer and coach—but they also offered me the opportunity to become a better person, father and husband.

Successful relationships begin by giving rather than by taking. Those who treat others the way they want to be treated themselves will quickly notice that this attitude makes all human interaction easy. My only regret is that I did not come across this coaching journey earlier in my life. I would have liked to use the above insights and learning points much sooner in my career as a manager. Who knows, certain things might have gone a lot more smoothly. However, as regrets don't get us anywhere, I thought of a way to make up for it: If I wanted to set things in motion and promote change in traditional work floor patterns, I could perhaps do so by spreading the message on a grand scale and that is why it has been such a pleasure to work on this book.

This adage by Persian poet Rumi (1207–1273) illustrates perfectly the heart of the matter:

> *"Yesterday I was clever, so I wanted to change the world.*
> *Today I am wise, so I am changing myself."*

ENDNOTES

1   J.M. Schwartz, M.D., and Sharon Begley. *The Mind & the Brain. Neuroplasticity and the Power of Mental Force*. ISBN 9780060988470
2   Luft J. and Ingham H. (1955). *The Johari Window: a graphic model for interpersonal relations*. University of California Western Training Lab
3   Bronnie Ware. *The Top Five Regrets of the Dying. A Life Transformed by the Dearly Departing* (2011)
4   Napoleon Hill & A. Pell. *Think and Grow Rich*. ISBN 9780449214923
5   Levinson, Daniel J. with Charlotte N. Darrow, Edward B. Klein, Maria H. Levinson and Braxton McKee. (1979) *The Seasons of a Man's Life*. ISBN 9780345282583
6   Marc Buelens, Ann Vermeiren. *Beter zorgen voor jezelf*. (2010). ISBN 9789020990393
7   Luc Dekeyser. Sociaal *agogische organisatieleer. Deel 1 – Leren kijken naar organisatie. Deel 2 – Veranderen van organisaties* (1991). ISBN 9053500707

This book was accomplished thanks to our thousands of hours of practical experience as professional coaches, and was also inspired by our colleagues at The Coaching Square:

Carole Warlop	Karen Kelchtermans	Monika De Crem
Damien Colmant	Kathleen Bosman	Nicole Wellens
Désirée Willems	Katrin Van Bladel	Patrick Zacharis
Dorothée Willems	Kris Vanhoof	Philippe Defaux
Els Van Laecke	Lilian Regeer	Philippe Vaneberg
Eva Pareyn	Magaly De Smet	Sybren Tuinstra
Jeanne van Dael	Marijke Van Moldergem	Veronique Meert

For more information:
BELGIUM   www.coachingsquare.be
NETHERLANDS   www.coachingsquare.nl
SWITZERLAND   www.coachingsquare.com

THE COACHING SQUARE